Selected by Tod Marshall,
Washington State Poet Laureate, 2016-2018

Sage Hill
P r e s s
Spokane, WA

WA129: Poets of Washington

ISBN: 978-0-9890359-0-3

First Printing, April 2017
Printed in the United States

For permissions and ordering information contact:
Sage Hill Press
1848 W. Bridge Ave
Spokane, WA 99201
or visit www.sagehillpoetry.com

Compiled and edited by Tod Marshall,
Washington State Poet Laureate, 2016-2018

Publisher: Thom Caraway
Managing Editor: Jeffrey G. Dodd
Associate Managing Editor: Megan Robinson
Assistant Managing Editor: Hailee Meyers
Interior Book Design: Megan Robinson
Cover Design: Jeffrey G. Dodd

This project was funded by the Washington State Poet Laureate
Program, a partnership of Humanities Washington and the
Washington State Arts Commission.

Contents

Tod Marshall	Editor's Note	1
Sherman Alexie	Tracks	5
Luther Allen	Midsummer on the West Side	7
Patients and Families at Seattle Children's Hospital and Elizabeth Austen	My Story Begins	8
Terry Bain	Tell Me About the Trees	10
Quenton Baker	Lurch	12
Julie Baldock	Freewheeling	15
Akesha Baron	Camano Island	16
Dawn Pichón Barron	LUCKY	17
James Bertolino	Dear Bigfoot	18
Linda Bierds	The Hive at Kew Gardens, 2016	19
Jennifer Boyden	Each Answer I Answer To	20
Anita Boyle	As Wild Geese Gather	21
Allen Braden	Where Were You When the Mountain Blew?	22
E. Hank Buchmann	Coming Summer	23
Catherine Bull	Albrecht Dürer Moves to Ilwaco, Washington	24
Jennifer Bullis	Claude Lévi-Strauss Paces the Beach at Point Whitehorn, Washington	26
D.S. Butterworth	Arriving at Mutiny Bay, October 19, 2013	27
Becky Carlson	Anacortes Fish Wife	28
Bill Carty	Poem in the Presidentiad	29
Claudia Castro Luna	Here Is Where We Are	30
Joanne Clarkson	The Girl Who Wore Cedar	31
Kevin Craft	Washaway Beach	32

Mary Eliza Crane	Sonnet in Yakima Canyon	34
Michael Daley	In Memory	35
LLyn De Danaan	Autumn on Oyster Bay	36
Alice Derry	Four Sonnets for the Elwha	37
Pat Dixon	Coal Train	39
Rachel Eggers	Yard Work	40
Lynne Ellis	Interurban Trail Berry Pickers	41
Susan J. Erickson	Thirteen Ways of Looking at a Map of Fort Warden	42
Laura Falsetti	Lament	44
Leija Farr	Drying Blood	45
Kathleen Flenniken	Recital in B Reactor	46
Mark J. Fuzie	The Story of My Cousin's Lazy Eye (Thanks to Roberto Avila Beltran)	47
Cate Gable	Seattle: The Crane	48
Tess Gallagher	Deer Path Enigma	49
Laura Gamache	Oyster Master Class	50
Angel Gardner	A Ballad for the Unclaimed Ones	51
Carolyn Gilman	Driving Home from Spokane	52
Sierra Golden	Cold Nights	53
Lenora Rain-Lee Good	Because It Is Waiilatpu,	54
Joseph Green	Boy on the Beach	55
Sally Green	Shank	56
Samuel Green	Belle de Boskoop	57
Jasleena Grewal	Stares Like Pins	58
Mark Halperin	Eagle	59
Robert Hasselblad	Postcard, January 1922	60
Irene Hayes	*Via Negativa*	61
Merna Ann Hecht	On Inviting Wendell Berry to Orting	62
Christine Hemp	Sounding	64
Rebecca Hoogs	Pioneer Square Pile Driver	65
Christopher Howell	A So-Called Respite	66

Penny K. Johnson	Women Glean Apples in Wapato	68
Isamu Jordan	Our Glass Can	70
Richard Kenney	And More Vivalding	71
Larry Kerschner	The Bee Dancer	72
Rachel Kessler	At the Ballard Locks Fish Ladder	73
Jason Kirk	Olympic Harvest A Haiku Sequence	74
Shelley Kirk-Rudeen	Psalms from the Palouse	75
Laurie Klein	Maple Grove	76
J.I. Kleinberg	Slough Music	77
Sarah Koenig	Tank	78
Robert Lashley	Elders Rage at the Water Spirits After a Shootout	79
Jenifer Browne Lawrence	Landscape with No Net Loss	80
Jenny Liou	Too Late	81
Eric Lochridge	Walla Walla Sweets	82
Priscilla Long	Nisqually Delta	83
Christopher Luna	From GHOST TOWN, USA Mill Plain Blvd. & Andresen Rd. 2/28/09	84
Vikram Madan	Mt. Rainier	85
Ruth Marcus	Dungeness Valley	86
Terry Martin	In Every Ripe, Ready Thing	87
Georgia S. McDade	The Mountain	88
Heather McHugh	52-Blue	89
Ross McMeekin	Where the Sun Goes Once It Sets	91
Maureen McQuerry	Starting Late in the Afternoon	92
Catherine Alice Michaelis	Ozette Beach	93
Kevin Miller	About George	94
Maria Rosa Mills	Haplotype	95
Karen Mobley	Spokane	96
Daniel Edward Moore	A Ghost Minority	97
Elizabeth Myhr	(Untitled)	98

Arlene Naganawa	Dear Mr. Cooke	99
Shankar Narayan	How to Run Above the Cliffs	100
Paul Nelson	97. Clues from Hell	102
Sierra Nelson	Influence	104
Duane Niatum	Sleeping Woman	105
Sheila Nickerson	Searching for the True Name of the Douglas Fir	106
Courtney Oldwyn	Run Out of Stock	107
Kristen Orlando	Another Angle	108
Nancy Pagh	Boom	109
Shin Yu Pai	Marine Science Center, Port Townsend	110
Carl Palmer	May 18th, 1980	111
Lucia Perillo	On the Chehalis River	112
Paul Piper	For Li Po	113
Anna Quinn	Communion	114
Ben Read	Coroner's Report	115
Laura Read	Colonel George Wright Shot 800 Horses Here	116
Philip H. Red Eagle	The Things We Carry Now	117
Susan Rich	This Is Why the Relationship Might Work	119
LeAnne Ries	Heidi	120
Katrina Roberts	Palouse Falls	121
Tom Robbins	Stick Indians	123
Janette Lyn Rosebrook	Attenuation	125
Rob Schlegel	Lucid Ruse	126
Lynn Rigney Schott	Solstice Song, Stevens County 2016	127
Betty Scott	A Catalogue of Things Given Up	128
Heidi Seaborn	What We Hold On To	129
Derek Sheffield	Blast and Surge	130
Martha Silano	At the Bybee Farms U-Pick, North Bend, Washington	131

Judith Skillman	**Your Scars**	132
Kathryn Smith	**Legends Say**	133
Ed Stover	**What Remains**	134
George Thomas	**Legacy**	135
Joanna Thomas	**Drinking Beer at the Goldendale Demolition Derby**	136
Sallie Tierney	**Point Hudson Light**	137
Anastacia-Renee Tolbert	**Bold**	138
John Whittier Treat	**Smallpox First Came to the Pacific Northwest in 1770**	139
Emily Van Kley	**Memorial**	140
Nance Van Winckel	**Ahem**	142
Connie Walle	**Precipitate**	143
Michael Dylan Welch and Tanya McDonald	**Rain into River**	144
Ellen Welcker	**Masters of Condescension**	145
John Whalen	**Naked People I Have Known #34**	146
Katharine Whitcomb	**Winter Saturday**	148
Bill Yake	**Great Uncle Erwin**	149
Judith Yarrow	**Oregon Mist**	150
Maged Zaher	**(Untitled)**	151
Maya Jewell Zeller	**The Doctor Asks Her to Describe It**	152
Acknowledgements		155
Contributors		157

Editor's Note

In January 2016, about a week before I began my service as Washington State Poet Laureate, an email appeared in my inbox; the message read, "Given that great composers and poets have crafted symphonies and verse to commemorate roads and bridges, we thought your voice would be a meaningful and memorable way to pay tribute to" …our state's largest transportation bill. I was being asked to write an occasional poem, a dedication to honor and to celebrate Washington's *largest transportation bill*. A bridge? Sure. A road? No problem. A bill? I hesitated. The event was a week away. I thought, "I need more time to make *my art*"—and then I realized how precious, how spoiled that attitude was, and I changed my mind and got to work, did what poets do, sat down, grabbed a pen and tried to pull words from the shimmering air:

There Are Many Ways to Move Through Our Day

Think of first tracks—to water, to crops, out to the blossoming garden
and even the latrine—trails to neighbors, shady groves along the river,
and secret berry patches, the grassiest meadows always just over
the mountains, across deep currents, the stretch of seeing:

think how first paths rut toward dirt roads, gravel, black pavement,
whoosh of car and car, lumbering bus and swaying semi-truck,
then wide freeways and finally airplane scribbles in the sky, the once dark
glowing with glittering satellites. Things change. Often

what's meant gets lost in that wide space, even as time zips quicker,
flash of a sent text, that new highway. Let words gather our heaviest loads,
meaning from many directions, and perhaps, today, we can remember

those first tracks toward water, first bridges, first trails to a meadow,
berry vines, and the lines that bind all of us. Sometimes, we can pick
our routes. We can choose to say connect and mean closer together.

—January 2016

More than a year has passed since that request and the subsequent event where I read the poem to dignitaries while construction crews stood near at hand, dressed as if they were ready to get to work that very afternoon, and that poem, in some ways, foreshadowed my service for our state, the driving over mountain passes, across sage-strewn stretches of I-90, up curving highways to Curlew and down twisty roads in the Palouse, on ferries and bridges, through thick traffic and wide-open lanes, on and on. I'm pleased to share that poetic effort as part of my introduction to the dozens of other poems in *WA 129*. These works— by award-winning writers and poets finding print for the first time— are a testament to our state's bountiful creativity and the ways that Washington's poets transform inspiration into memorable language.

And those ways *are* myriad! Our state has so many poets writing a wide variety of poetries: from long narrative poems and wacky surrealist romps to sprawling-lined diatribes and pithy lyrics that pop! We have stage poets exploring the boundaries of the page, and we have sonneteers stretching the edges of that accentual-syllabic pattern. We also have vibrant slam scenes, wonderful publishers, and many festivals aimed solely at celebrating the power of poetry (in Seattle, Spokane, Tieton, Wenatchee, Ellensburg, Skagit Valley, Bellingham, and many other places). Simply, we have many people invested in exploring and sharing how language matters. This anthology is, I hope, an embodiment of and contribution to that enthusiasm, engagement, and prolific word-energy. In my service at this position, I have heard Washington singing, and that voice is diverse, stirring, and compelling. Herein are some of its songs.

Over two thousand poems were submitted from writers throughout our state. Although many of the poems mention Washington places and people and icons (mountains, rivers, place names, and salmon— lots and lots of salmon), some of the poems journey outside of our state's borders and even outside of our cultural moment. I did my best to choose a wide range of voices, subjects, and poetics; in this book, you'll find poignant elegies, powerful eclogues, snappy sonnets, incisive haiku, memorable dirges, and light-hearted verses that might bring forth a smile; simply, I tried to gather, as Whitman put it, the "varied caroling" of poets in our state—the "lines" that show our glorious differences and the lines that might also connect us. I hope that readers enjoy this book. I have been honored to represent our state, to work on behalf of Humanities Washington and Arts WA, and to receive such a warm welcome from so many writers and literary enthusiasts. If these poems give pleasure, challenge visions, and maybe even bring about a sharp pang of literal, emotional, or intellectual recognition, then I trust readers can join me in my confidence that we are fortunate to live in a state rich with both poetry and inspiration.

Sincerely,

Tod Marshall
Washington State Poet Laureate,
2016-2018

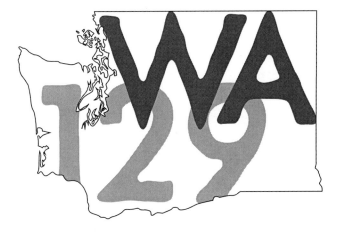

Tracks

Sherman Alexie

My back is too injured to drive
So I ride the Amtrak from Seattle to Portland—
A short jaunt past barely dormant volcanoes—
But I rent a small sleeping compartment

So I can lie flat during the four-hour trip.
I fall asleep, of course, and dream
Of my ancestors, those Spokane Indians
Who still fished for wild salmon.

Those wild salmon are ghosts now.
As are my ancestors. But what did
My grandparents think when they first saw
A locomotive? Did they know

Those trains would change everything?
They would bring millions of white people.
They would bring the wood and metal
And wire. They would bring heat

And electricity and books and alien
Fruits and vegetables. I imagine my grandparents
Grew to hate the trains. I imagine their ghosts
Hate the trains, too. But I am one indigenous man

Who has forgiven the past. Well, I've forgiven
Trains, at least. Or maybe I love
Trains now because they are still loud
And they have grown old. These trains

Are the grandparents of those cars
On the highway and those airplanes in the sky.
These trains are always threatened to be replaced
With something faster, something more sleek

And contemporary. But I love the slow roll
Along the tracks. I love the frequent stops.
I love the way these trains have barely changed.
So, maybe, if something new lasts long enough,

Then it becomes something ancient and sacred.
Maybe this train is my grandmother. After all,
My train cradles me as I sleep. It holds me
In one calm and dark place, as everybody else

Quickly streams from one place to the next.
Oh, Grandmother Train, I know I rarely visit,
But I still need you. Next time, I will ride with you
Over a river that is still filled with wild salmon.

Grandmother, we'll sing through every switch and detour.
We'll praise all of those good things that somehow endure.

Midsummer on the West Side

Luther Allen

beyond in all directions, fire.
no snowpack and summer started in april.

young thimbleberries, salmonberries. brown. dead.
more and less of every insect.

the bears are already down, hungry.
wells go dry. winds shift and

haze, smoke-smell from a hundred miles away.
a nervousness. an edge. to everything.

if this was just smudge, the blessing of sage.
but none of us can pray as long as we used to.

as we need to. there is much to imagine.
to fear. if that trigger is pulled here.

My Story Begins

A collaborative poem, written by patients and families
at Seattle Children's Hospital and Elizabeth Austen

My story begins with a dream of a child,
    travel suitcases and hazy flights,
        a small-town girl moving to a big city,

putting on my tap shoes,
    keeping the faith,
        dancing.

My story begins with Cambodia,
    leaving Cleveland, leaving Hawaii, flying
        to Disneyland, swinging

from monkey bars, running a mile
    in pouring rain. My story begins
        with four words: Your child has cancer.

We found a large mass in his liver.
    Heart failure.
        My story begins in heartbreak and fear.

And my story begins with Allah,
    God, Jesus, Muhammad.
        Oh, hail Mary, full of grace.

My story begins with a brave 3-year-old,
    the power of prayer, the power of faith,
        singers in bands, the love and blessings of friends and family,

our two beautiful daughters, an open mind,
    a 14-year-old with the heart of a champion.
        Ramon! Liam! Lloyd!

Quentin, TJ, hope!
    Brady, Damian, Samantha,
        Jason, Luis, love!

Carolyn, Danielle, Connor, Jamay,
    Elise, Tanner, Ahmie, Howard,
        Jesus, Jesus, Jesus.

My story begins with hope in God,
    forgiveness,
        compassion.

My story begins with waking up,
    beating the odds,
        a new heart.

And my story begins with a walk in the woods,
    helping others, caring, sharing, grace and humility,
        a new beginning.

The chirp of a bird, a teeny tiny hummingbird,
    puppies, a polar bear,
        a black-footed ferret.

Cake! (o joy).
    A chocolate mint sundae with strawberry sprinkles!
        Strategically placed doilies. A rainbow waffle.

My story begins with
    Oops, I forgot my belt,
        a bright white smile.

A dream of a freckled girl humming a halo.
    A song.
        Love.

My story begins with the volcano.
    The river.
        The heart.

Tell Me About the Trees

Terry Bain

Not about the trees but
the trees.

Tell me about the trunks and the pitch and
the leaves. The bark. And the shape.
Where the birds live.
About the cones and the whirlygigs
and pollen. Say deciduous and coniferious.
Unexpectedly pronounce the "h"
in "herbacious." Just for me.

Tell me about roots and soil.
Wildlife. Squirrels.
Explain what a cache is,
and what I can expect to find there
if I dig it out with my hands.
Tell me again.

About shade. About autumn.
About rain and moss and
clearcuts.
Fire.

Chainsaw, cordwood, and pickup.
Robin, sparrow, starling.
Flicker, crow, cat.
Termites and ants.
Tell me
about ants.

Tell me about my mother. Where you
carved her name and why.
Tell me about the trees
—not about the trees,
but the trees.

Sit up and get out of this bed.
Tell me again.
Right now.
Please.

Lurch

Quenton Baker

for Porter Moss

Maybe a gasket blew.
Maybe this Tennessee July
is too thick to drive through.
And Lord knows how many miles
that engine has on it.
No matter.
Nothing to do but grab the luggage
and hump it to the Dickson railroad station.

So, the mighty Memphis Red Sox
walk the walk,
end up piled in an already full car.
No room to separate, thumbed
into the vestibule with the overflow,
white and black alike.
It's hot, everyone feels stuck
under the sun's tongue.
Nothing to do but bear it—
dark is a long way off.

Inevitably, a dice game is struck up.
One white boy is carrying on
harder than the rest
yelling about the roll
grabbing a few women's backsides.
He's already had a few and still having,
his shirt more whiskey and sweat than cotton.

The train stops.
Sign outside says McEwen.
The redcap comes in
grabs the rowdy boy
by his collar, informs him of his early exit.
The white boy bucks.

Pulls a piece from his waist
and levels it.
Now the conductor comes in, ready with his.
The raucous boy relents
takes his leave.
Everyone in the vestibule
starts breathing again.
The train rolls on
then *crack! crack! crack!*
The white boy lets off from the platform.
Random. Blind.
Nobody's hit
except Porter Moss.
You see, they call him Ankleball Moss
on account of his delivery:
low as low can get, he slurs that thing
right off the top of an ant's head
knuckles buzzing the ground.
The best submariner anyone's ever seen:
gutshot.
Moss is hollering for a doctor
but nothing can be done until the next town.
Them boys clear as much air as they can,
lay down their Red Sox uniforms
for Moss to bleed on.

Dark is settled in now.
Some are grateful for the abated heat
some don't notice.
The train pulls in to Waverly.
Them boys told:
sorry, ain't no doctor
or hospital for him here.

The train pulls out.
Moss lurches with the car
nothing to be done until the next town.

The train pulls in to Bruceton.
White doctor gets on board,
shoots some mercy into Moss
and says:
sorry, ain't no hospital for him here.

The train pulls out.
Moss lurches with the car.
Midnight now,
everything outside
wrapped in a black wing.
Nothing to be done until the next town.

The train pulls in to Lexington.
Them boys told:
sorry, ain't no doctor
or hospital for him here.

The train pulls out.
Moss lurches with the car.
Nothing to be done until the next town.

The train pulls in to Jackson.
Them boys told:
ambulance coming.
Now the sun's coming too.
They load Moss in,
leaving the uniforms in the vestibule
wet with ten hours of Ankleball's blood.
Them boys follow the sirens
to the first hospital that anyone has
for a bleeding giant.

Freewheeling

Julie Baldock

Years ago,
when we were still so young
I took pictures
of the things I saw when I wasn't with you
so you would know where I came from,
and where I was heading.
I pushed the lens of the Polaroid against
scratched bus windows,
laid little squares on the seat next to me,
watched buildings grow from nothing.
The Twin Towers still stood
and I clicked and caught
them before they fell.
I remember the disconnect the next week,
sitting next to you on our mattress on the floor
in our one-room apartment in First Hill,
moving the rabbit ears to try to see something
more horrible than we had ever seen before,
trying to reconcile what we were making
with what the world seemed
intent to destroy.
And I think about this now,
while taking phone pictures of snowy woods
to send you hours away.
I try to write it out so you can see my vision still,
my fingers sticky with clementine juice,
leaving tiny prints on the paper
as my pen jumps,
leaving each dent on the road in the fiber.
Highways and byways,
bumpy roads and dirty windows,
still so much more to see.

Camano Island

Akesha Baron

Peter waters the small lettuces. The tulips
give themselves up utterly, all around.

"When you need a cocktail, just raise your hand."
I ask if he always lights the candles on the Guadalupe shrine.

"Definitely when the tulips are blooming like this." The Dutch
bulbs festoon every surface indoors, adorned in vases.

He sits in front of the lit wood stove in the morning, pointing
out seals swimming by. I'm reminded of a morning in

Mexico. The slight chill and the smell of wood
smoke. All the white light. Coffee in a yellow cup.

A life of cloth and wood without many surfaces for
fingerprints to accumulate. A little bit of dirt in everything.

Any fish is tiny, dried and salted. Any lamp
that lights up at night is a sign of progress.

LUCKY

Dawn Pichón Barron

Years ago when given my first and only *escapulario*, the thin string around my neck holding a miniature cloth picture of the mother of all, the Mexican woman down the street told me to tuck it beneath my shirt—keep it pressed to my skin for protection. *Everyone like us must wear one,* she whispered.

Family Polaroids: three boys with dirty blonde hair and pale limbs surround a girl with eyes and hair the color of mud and skin, a stick of cinnamon.

In the rural outskirts of the Inland Empire, a school official knocked on the front door, holding a free-lunch form. Asked if my name meant sun rising, if I was adopted.

Every Halloween friends told me to be Pocahontas. With my beauty mark, I chose Gypsy. Once, I was a ghost.

During junior high, I moved to shaded areas, avoiding the greasy bottles of baby oil as others slathered and placed tinfoil reflectors on their pale bellies.

In high school, the driver's ed teacher snapped the seatbelt across my chest, *Bet you're a feisty one with that dark skin.* He scheduled my drives alone—so I could get more practice.

As a young adult, sitting across from a man I just met who had the same hair, eyes, and skin as me, I remembered my mom telling me *you just tan real good, so count yourself lucky.*

Away at college, my best friend complimented me: *You almost look like a white girl, just with brown skin.*

A boyfriend, hands caressing my bare skin, murmured how he loved the color of me: *cafe con leche, madrone bark, his little chestnut.* I brushed his hands away. Feeling ghost.

Dear Bigfoot

James Bertolino

I'm sending you this message
to deny that I am deceased.
However, as the general consensus
would have it, I may be, like you,
extinct. What I was as an active, younger man
no longer exists. That life is gone.
Now when I look into a thriving, green-faced
pond, I am comforted by both the microscopic
and tangible life. When my eyes climb
the slim, angled legs of the heron,
then move from the point of its long beak
to beautiful, round eyes that do not
hesitate to stare back at me, I bless
that bird as it flaps its large, somewhat awkward
wings. I am present in this world,
and the world is present in me.
My belief does not require that I fold
my hands in prayer.
I, too, am blessed.

The Hive at Kew Gardens, 2016

Linda Bierds

[I am now working on] my mathematical theory of embryology...
symmetrical structures...flowers...leaf arrangement...
–Alan Turing, 1951

From a distance, it seems
the thinnest of funnel clouds, or—yes—
all the land's bees swarming.
But this is the art of science and we are inside it—
a forty-ton honeycomb of air and aluminum wire.
A latticed sculpture, seventeen meters high.
Bend closer, someone says—we can almost see,
in the meadow below us, the tiny, living hive
that sets these wires humming.
And now we are holding between our lips
flat, almost weightless wooden sticks
that, touched to the lattice, transfer the bees' language
through the bones of our heads: the piping and begging,
the tooting and quacking....And how is it done,
this invisible relay, bee to vibration to us?
You would have loved the circuitry, those smallest
of sounds, tucked deep in a flowering hedge,
swelling upward and outward
to fill a hiveful of stick-biting minds.
And far below us, the inflorescence you tracked,
stem to stem, the leaves, one, one, two, three,
the codes that set the shapes, the clicks that set
them ticking. There and there,
the marigolds lift their flattened crowns
like trays of the smallest flowers.
Capitulae. Bend closer,
we can sip through our wooden,
tubal tongues the most ancient of grammars—
and although the dance will be hidden from us,
we can follow along through the piping.

Each Answer I Answer To

Jennifer Boyden

The heron is a tall window. When I am done looking
through it, I will need to answer
for how I have used the world.

Until then, the trees are content at the edge
of a window like that: watery, unasked for.
What do I have to tell the heron?

That hunger must answer
to the unpicked field of blackberries.
That the fish tossed on the side of the road
had never answered air in such abundance,
breath pulled like a bone from flesh.
That the sun is the one who asked
the heron to invent stillness.

Above, another cloud loosens a broken corner
of sky.

The heron watches what swims within
in its own shadow: mirror likeness
of the darkness it can see through
to what it will live by.

It is sharpening its knives of intention,
inseparable from how
I should thank the grass
while I am here.

As Wild Geese Gather

Anita K. Boyle

This gentle place—where cool, gray mist meets the hushed, rough-hewn fields—
carries the whistling wings of wood ducks rushing from the pond,
and the scraggling of the heron, as she, too, hurries home
to the damaged cedar over the brim of horizon.

This gentle place—where cool, gray mist meets the hushed, rough-hewn fields—
has always been home. Rabbits and deer are welcomed by black-
berry knolls, hanks of canary grass, and pink feral roses.

This is the place where I will lie down on the dampening
ground, to soak up the earth's sweet music in the afterlight.
This gentle place, where cooling gray greets the rough-hewn fields.

Where Were You When the Mountain Blew?

Allen Braden

The voice on the radio continues,
"Stay inside. Stay put. Stay calm."
Katie hugs her knees up to her chest,
"I wish he'd stop saying that."
The voice on the radio.
Outside a cloud of bark dust
swells the loafing shed. The voice.
Our feeder cattle and milk cows
storm in and out. The sky
tingles. The voice continues.
Our breath filling with grit,
sand or soot? No, sulfuric
ash raining darkly.
The voice on the radio.
Patches, Old Catahoolie
and the rest of our pets
crowd in on the porch.
The radio. The voice.
Sunday morning darkens,
continuing its instruction.

Coming Summer

E. Hank Buchmann

For Rebecca

she smells wood smoke at night
dreaming she is a child again
beach pines and ocean rain

now she is a desert dweller, where
long shadows cross the big land
beneath squadrons of stratus clouds

he watches her with the shovel
squaring the edges of a new hole
home for centerpiece hornbeams

hammered stakes outline her dreams
here it will be, there it will be
a quarrel between vigor and repose

it is the eve of coming summer
a slanting of toil against sunset
where birches flame in the gloaming

water beads off the new grass
a shimmering parcel of emeralds
befitting the pulse of nightfall

he cannot command his eyes
to look away, fearing he will miss
the fixed beauty she adds to twilight

Albrecht Dürer Moves to Ilwaco, Washington

Catherine Bull

Dürer would have seen a reason for living
in a town like this, with eight stranded whales
to look at, with the sweet sea air coming into your house
on a fine day, from water etched
with waves as formal as the scales
on a fish or the thumbprints in a thick dictionary.
What charter boats there still are,
captained by the Sea Hag Tavern patrons,
by Rockys and Ray-Rays,
go out past the dredge spoils,
the unfortunate view in front of the view,
out into the mighty currents that cross-hatch
to black on not-fine days. The boats are white
or white and one other color,
named for the most part with poor puns.

Despite this, Dürer would have seen reason for living
in Ilwaco: the updated Horsemen,
Recession, Meth, Obesity, and Debt,
flying grotesque up and down the peninsula
with flocks of birds who demonstrate mathematical principles
back and forth in lines over the breakers,
hiccuping glissandos that flurry-rise and clot,
shimmer, diminish, carriage-return,
running-start glide, up-ladder and tip
over the air over the waves.

Lottery luck is unheard of
in a town like this with eight whales stranded
in the upper third of a gloomy mural,
faded to pastel already, on the side of the fire station
that replaced the fire station
which burned down. At Thanksgiving the Christmas tree
made out of crab pots stacked in a pyramid
and wound with big colored lights,
is ceremoniously plugged in.
On Saturdays, May to September,
there is a farmers market where you can buy
lotion with healing properties, speckled eggs,
flowers in shocking colors Dürer never used,
and photographs of sunsets you could hang at home
to look at, so the salted air
might come into your house somewhere else.
But though they are real they look fake.

There is a bookstore, and Ole Bob's
for fresh fish and fish tacos,
idle galleries, idle canneries,
a bank/pharmacy combination drive-through
and a wine bar where you can hear sometimes
jazz musicians string cat's cradles
through the tiny audience and move them
from pattern to pattern. And, perpetually,
as formal as the scales
on a fish, precise, dark-green and black
instead of silver and blue-green
are Cape Disappointment's pine trees,
pointy and thick, with tops like steeple stars
which, where they haven't been cleared for huge houses, stand
for hope, and burr the intersecting lines
of sky and land, and land and water,
and home and visitor.

Claude Lévi-Strauss Paces the Beach at Point Whitehorn, Washington

Jennifer Bullis

Mythical thought always progresses from the awareness of oppositions to their resolution.
—Claude Lévi-Strauss, *Structural Anthropology*

The ocean's voice silences all others—
hush, hush—speaking wind as its myth
of origin. Between waves, I hear

the phonemes *gneiss, schist, gneiss*:
the land and the Salish Sea exchanging
beach stones to enact their kinship.

But what mediating element resolves
the opposition between life and death?

I see trickster Raven everywhere,
shifting shapes, reconciling prey and predator,
scavenging both into himself.

And here, the ritual of salmon is casting a coho
awash on the shore. Already it has exchanged
its life for the lives of its daughters and sons.

It struggled from Cascade creek to river to ocean
and returned: the structure of every story
of going out and coming back.

I see death and life synthesize in the telling
of salmon swimming away and home,
of the ocean voicing *forth, back, forth.*

Arriving at Mutiny Bay, October 19, 2013

D.S. Butterworth

The sleeping bags and pillows, binoculars,
novels, laptops, the old pawn-shop guitar,
bottled water, and groceries almost seem
the reason we come to the cabin. Maybe
we need to learn again the weight
of our needs. When the wind calms
the bay's inventory tells us, No:
mergansers, loons, golden eyes, heron
and grebe, scaup, widgeon, Dahl's
porpoises, salmon leaping franticly.
The far shore and freighters are lost
in fog but these limits say the inner
bay is enough. A cormorant scarecrows
its wings to dry and we move closer.
Then it dives to resurface with a bullhead
bigger than its own head, swallows
it whole and alive, and we move to the edge.
Then the enormity of the grey opens up
and levels us, the day's huge roundhouse
blow to the cranium. Our eyes hollow
out and the grey obliterates us and we
are here because we aren't us anymore
having entered the other necessity,
the wordless weight of necessary grey
so close to the blank edge of things.

Anacortes Fish Wife

Becky Carlson

Crates of various sizes stacked in our garage—
Symbols for our approaching goodbye;
All those things you or the crew
Could want or need on the fishing grounds.

For twenty-one years
My internal clock has gone off every spring.
I hate your perennial absence;
Your nagging call of the sea.

Surge of my blood
Against the sure shore of your leaving;
Surf-like scrape of my missing you;
The push-pull of mornings—days—months.

You've been on autopilot all these years;
I have no rights in this matter of fish.
From the dock I watch the froth of your white wake.
Deep throm-throm of powerful Cat-engine—
Chasing bluebacks—then pinks—knowing
The run peaks when the salmonberries are ripe.

Poem in the Presidentiad

Bill Carty

Too scared this morning
to reverse from the driveway,
we throttled through the garage
and lost transmission
in a field where four snow
geese buried their necks
in muck, low afternoon light
in the furrows, a poultice
of turmeric and pain,
which echoed from the barn
because the barn is a singing
thing. Back to the city.
It's Friday. Everyone
who listens to country music
with the windows down
got off early today. The beach
isn't open to the public anymore.
Towels pile at the gate. We
can still smell the coal train
as we duck beneath
the skeleton of its conveyance,
tracks where someone
wrote *sueños* three times
on the trestle. Someone
was unafraid to spend
all their wishes. Nightfall.
Mosquitoes eat what we offer,
the little flesh to be found
in the statuary where we walk
after dinner, never having moved
less like two objects and more like the weather.

Here Is Where We Are

Claudia Castro Luna

I have always
wanted a house
with a big porch
said my friend
on our walk
this morning
that way I can sit,
drink my coffee
and watch
the rain
fall

The Girl Who Wore Cedar

Joanne Clarkson

For Judy

We were the same age
when I saw her as the forest
soft-skinned steps
matching the other dancers.
She wore the dress
her father's mother wove,
cedar bark harvested
in strips, seamed with sinew,
beaded. Among drums

she lost her shyness. Grade
behind me in school, I knew
her by one name only. Had seen
her on the playground
giggling with friends
her green sweater, pleated
skirt the same plaid

as mine. One afternoon
I tutored her in math.
Long division. Her tan fist
moist against lined paper.
Pencil eraser bitten
to the metal. She said
nothing as I solved for dividends.
At the end of the hour
she wrote a number. We were

never friends although we
walked the same road home
until the final Y. And after
the Longhouse dance I dared
to say See you where
my way led through fir
and hers under cedar.

Washaway Beach

Kevin Craft

A thing so fragile
be careful what you name it.
Call it tenderness or
it takes a village,
how quaint the ancient art
of holding hands, speaking into tin
cans strung together or
making plans to be something
somewhere else next year like driftwood
in a rolling breaker,
trunk by trunk the forest
swallowed up by rain or hunger only endlessness
can carry, no more forest looming
for the trees.

Who can say we didn't see it coming?
First it took the lighthouse, the clam cannery,
the cove that covered nothing with its name:
North Cove. Shoalwater. Grayland gravy.
Wave by wave it took the school, the post office,
the Grange Hall's low uneasy scuttlebutt
hurried out to empty parking lots,
threatening now the highway north and south.

Call in the engineers.
If the subject is memory
we've hardly lived there but the book
vanishes with every turned page,
sand in the mouth of the river,
grit in the eye of the sleeper,
slow churn of the tidal channel
changing hands with *sturm und drang*.
The story of the littoral is one arrival
reiterating its gritty salutation
so far off at first it's hard to hear
aright like dunes in ruin, skeleton of a shipwreck
emerging from the hourglass, gulls given
to laughter fierce as anything going—

*

call it hard luck or love thy neighbor if nothing else
will save us from forgetting
sanderling and sea wrack, the ground
we took for granted giving way.

Sonnet in Yakima Canyon

Mary Eliza Crane

In afternoon play of light and shadow
across the canyon, the pale-green flush
of early grass, muted blue
of new grown sage, and yellow flash
of balsamroot are scrutinized
in the watchful gaze of bighorn sheep.
Sure-footed, bounding through the scree,
quench their thirst at a mountain creek.

This scene should be eternal, but it's not,
though its history is written on the rocks
in ocher, black and gold, for anyone
who cares to learn the language.
There's truth if not beauty in the knowledge
that nothing turns out quite the way we thought.

In Memory

Michael Daley

Seamus Heaney appeared to me last night,
'flicker-lit,' here beside the cool Skagit
where chatter of the kingfisher's heard most
beside a highway hollow as the mist,
apparition from whom I learn to read
on this silt bank where I believe the dead.
He says at two 'Quads' music streams two ways
then he's shushed by a hushed afterlife nurse.
On a map the river, a root-twined nerve,
gouged glacier slopes, polished as poetry.
Once in a hall he tuned to such a glow
I heard him admire as 'vegetative'
that tendril-soaked turf of early Roethke,
and woke, to sleep, too soon to see him go.

Autumn on Oyster Bay

LLyn De Danaan

The fir branch, heavy with last night's rain,
bows deeply to applauding gulls,
salutes a heron.
She pokes and prods the low tide mud
while raccoons clam.

Four Sonnets for the Elwha

Alice Derry

After reading Tony Hoagland essays

The poetry of earth is never dead.
—John Keats

As in the old stories, taking a wrong turn
on the trail, I discover the magic bonanza:
thirty calypso orchids, a bank of fawn lilies.
My lover's stayed home and can't mind
how extravagantly I kiss my hand
to the giant trillium as I meet them.
Hello, my lovelies. Hello, my sweets,
me wandering lonely as a cloud.
Grouse thump their mating call.
I'll never catch up, but twice
I've almost bumped into deer.
No screaming. No terrified leaping.
We stared and went on. Just ahead,
a flicker's orange rust disappears.

Once I've found the bank above the river
I'm looking for, I'll tear open a sandwich
of bread I made last night and jam
poured in its jars last summer from berries
like those blooming now, right here—
not just because I want to follow
the path from hand to mouth:
I like to make jam. I like to knead bread.
Letting words, yeasty and strange,
rise toward the hearing of them:
break, braid, abandon, brandish:
sun on this spot where I took the last of it
in the fall, what was going, now leafing,
buzz-cut of light green on the alders.

While I lie full length in the grass and heat,
a single thread of thrush notes trails
across the firs. Raven wings his shadow
close in, to check what I'm eating.
This mountain river gives my town its water.
I tip my bottle up, waiting with the rest,
just months until century-old dams
come down. We're luring the salmon back.
Miles ahead, at the suspension bridge,
water's white sound carves the swath of beach
my daughter and I stumbled on last summer.
Surrendering our salami sandwiches
to the yellow jackets, we let icy current
slide us along—as if possibility existed.

I can't help it. On this day after the banishment
of nature poems, everything stands
still for me: a snake corded red and yellow
stretched motionless in the quick heat
except for its seeing tongue;
mourning cloak sheltering from the wind
where I can look my fill; across the river
fifteen elk cows, grazing or lying ruminant.
I'd forgotten how stonecrop
climbs rose and sage up the basalt walls
and among it, the quiet lavender of broomrape,
shaded perfectly to ignite its hosts' colors,
belying its name, its parasitic
preying on what is green and making.

Coal Train

Pat Dixon

A month ago winter slid out a sunny Saturday door
and we went along, to the Columbia River Gorge
where tilled fields and waterfall mists
filled the air with the scent of moist earth.

The spring sun was warm as we drove a late
afternoon highway lined with chartreuse-tinted
bushes and trees; the road wound between hills,
and the river glittered back the blue above.

We crept up on a freight train plowing west to the coast,
only a few miles an hour slower than we were driving,
hopper car after hopper car, filled with glistening black coal.
We paced them for miles, for dozens of miles,
until I wished I'd been counting the cars so I could tell
the story accurately, but I hadn't. It was surprising
how many there were. By the time the sun set,
the train and road were all we saw;
the blue sky paled above that race.

The road finally turned from the tracks,
the green of spring slipped back into the branches,
the gorge didn't appear so pure,
and the world lost a little more of its magic.

Our smiles faded;
we faced forward in the front seats,
oblivious to the invisible exhaust following us
as we exhaled the rest of the way home.

Yard Work

Rachel Eggers

Know this: I am alone
too much,

and I am a performer.
The scarf goes around my head two,
three times, for the benefit of surrounding fences.

The pitchfork is suitably rustic,
piercing leaf arms, leaf hearts—
I must push them away with brambly fingers,
pulsating hot beneath earth-tarnished gloves.

Still: it's nice,
the down-up and side-to-side.
The sky's a bowl overturned,
eking milky blueness.
Around the trees' bellies curl a ribbon of fire,
and the dogs go running round like plots of bad physics.

Interurban Trail Berry Pickers

Lynne Ellis

Pretty girls in white denim shorts hold
milk-glass bowls against their pin-pricked thighs.

One lifts her arm towards black fruit
and leans *en pointe* into the bramble.

Blind to the brush of wine-smack smears
on her denim, she pulls summer's stems.

Fruit upon fruit fills the curve at her hip.
She tiptoes on a forgotten campsite flop—

unmindful of the rumpled gray socks and empties
discarded beneath her coral toenails.

Thirteen Ways of Looking at a Map of Fort Warden

Susan J. Erickson

I.

The power of water and waves
is reduced
to three squiggly lines.

II.

I am of two minds to note
Bliss Vista perches
above Harbor Defense Way.

III.

The sound of bagpipes kilts through the summer air,
but is absent from the schematic pantomime.

IV.

A flagpole and a sculpture
are two circles.
A flagpole and a sculpture and a phone
are three circles.

V.

Is it irony
or evidence of evolutionary development
that a poetry press for peace
is headquartered on a former military base?

VI.

The quadrangle with the non-com houses
is cornered by brig, gym,
the blacksmith and mule bar.
The officer's housing overlooks
the tennis courts and parade grounds.

VII.

Oh, mapmaker without a name,
why do you label the north and south wings
of Building 204, but leave east and west
of others unmarked?

VIII.

I married a Marine
loyal to the motto of the *corps*.
But I know, too,
that *semper fi*
is the way he loves.

IX.

A map is a test of faith
when its scale is based on convenience
or undersized paper.

X.

At the military cemetery
I read Lisel Mueller's poem
"Missing the Dead" to my largest audience to date.
The dead hover in the crisp light
not even sighing at her words.

XI.

On the graves of infants
I leave winged maple seeds
because it seems the right thing to do.

XII.

The chapel is locked.
The unlocked chapels are all around us.

XIII.

When a map is put to paper
it raises questions
of attention and intention.
Every map is a translation.

Lament

Laura Falsetti

Again I wake to the flutter of sparrows in my mouth.

They seek refuge from the suffocating ash
that coats the planet. Rivers dwindle to ribbons
of sludge. Wetland trees, stripped and wretched
behind my house, are all that remain to bear witness.

In a shiny kettle from another life
I brew wild-mushroom tea
to the steady drip of the kitchen faucet.

When the new moon we've been anticipating
rises on the thirteenth, I watch her
from my bedroom window.
I see that she is screaming.

I ask her what she knows about the sparrows.

Like any love story, she says,
each civilization designs its own end.

Drying Blood

Leija Farr

The year his magic was stolen. I read recently that a new organ was found in the body. Wondered if that's where his body was allowed to hide inside himself a little more. Did he know he was music? His smile was a song we can't extract from us. In some ways, his smile was a song you listen to a handful of times to decipher.

That year they made a knot and a noose of his soul. They saw magic in the fact that his ghost still had a shadow. I saw the melanin pull from his cheekbones into the wind. Stretch itself thin and fly away. Black boys have learned not to scream, learned that this pain is mandatory.

Bullets pounding canvas, smoke embalming bodies. And the burning. The burning. His stomach was filled with the backwash of flames. The sun granted his last wish and that was that though his body was decaying he still glow, he still shine, he still be drowned in light. What is a Black boy if not light, if not the sun?

That year, he looked in the mirror and rewrote himself slave instead of king. If only he knew he was a king. I remember his tall frame, his precision, remember he opened the sky in his dreams and said heaven tastes like candy. Said it feels like home before it was gentrified.

I remember the war that year. How revolution could be seen dripping in each poem I wrote, I wrote about him. Wanted him to live. Wanted his body not be cracked open. Wanted my stanzas to personify into his shield.

I recall how I wore his obituary like a stain on my fingers for weeks. Remember that summer they painted the steps with his blood and it dried into a stain we forgot by the fall.

Recital in B Reactor

Kathleen Flenniken

Mid-Columbia Mastersingers, October 2, 2016

To take its measure—

> the 40-foot high graphite core,
> Panel-lit pressure gauges and thermocouples
> in each of 2,004 process tubes,
> Galvanometers and Beckman meters,
> cold-water manifolds, pile-discharge chutes,
>
> zones of impact and comparative aftermaths,
> 40,000 to 80,000 dead,
> permanent shadows burned into Nagasaki's streets,
> kimono patterns into long-ago skin—

a choir of 24 human voices sing,
24 lit faces
set against the old reactor's looming front face—
> an intricately-wrought mathematics
> become an engineered and finely-milled altarpiece—
>
> *Agnus Dei, qui tollis peccata mundi, miserere nobis*
> *Agnus Dei, qui tollis peccata mundi, miserere nobis*
> *Agnus Dei, qui tollis peccata mundi, dona nobis pacem*

petitioning the Lamb of God for peace and mercy
with mounting fervor until
with a sweep of the director's arms
they cease.

In the sudden suspended rest
of Barber's *Agnus Dei* measure 53,
we find not the silence we expect
but the reverberations of B Reactor
like an ancient cathedral speaking:

> What humankind has made here
> is mightier than all your breath.

The Story of My Cousin's Lazy Eye (Thanks to Roberto Avila Beltran)

Mark J. Fuzie

My mother has stage four, peritoneal cancer.
She fights hard.
She's halfway through round two with
Honorable and well-thought-of
Medicine. I call this warrior healing.

But maybe I should take her to Ohanapecosh
To the hot springs of Ohanapecosh
To the healing, mineral hot springs of Ohanapecosh
The magical healing hot springs of Ohanapecosh
Maybe we should walk the many steps to Ohanapecosh.

My cousin did once, to cure his lazy eye.
He walked the many steps to Ohanapecosh
Bathed in the healing mineral waters of Ohanapecosh
Sipped of its healing waters; washed his lazy eye
In the healing springs, the healing waters of Ohanapecosh.

His lazy eye woke up. It looked around at
What it had become. It began to get strong.
It began to believe in itself. It got ambition.
It picked up a backpack and walked the
Wonderland trail, all 93 miles—in ten days.

It moved to Seattle, then to L.A.
Where this once lazy eye became
A Sunday-morning news talk-show political pundit.
With its clear vision, it predicted a Trump Presidency,
The only pundit in all America to do so.

My cousin's normal eye saw this, and doubted itself.
It began to think this way, "I don't have vision.
I am not good enough." It took up the bottle,
Illicit drugs. But one day when its
Aqueous humor was nearly drained, it remembered.

And so, my cousin walked the many steps back
To the healing, mineral hot springs of Ohanapecosh.

Seattle: The Crane

Cate Gable

some weeks later
took itself apart
after putting
itself together—

conveniently,
we could follow suit,
readying our atoms
for death's reboot.

Deer Path Enigma

Tess Gallagher

For Jane Mead

Stepping where they step
in the unhindered woods
where my neighbor and I agreed not
to build a fence,
I startle the lone doe
from her kingdom of solitude.

Days since, she informs every hidden cavity
of fern and vine with possible
trespass—but also profound stillness
I crave when she fails
to appear. A light-footed yearning
inhabits me, though it was

blundering that flushed beauty
out. I lay down
my cities, rivers bereft
of their banks, snow-melt
and downpour where she pressed
the un-surrendered harp
of her body against moss. Vaults

of cement crack open. An arbor of blustering
neon goes dark in the borderland
of word-wrecked freedoms. Out of this
over-lay of the human, the doe
uncoils herself with power
that is not retreat, just

the nothing-else-that-could-happen,
as my uninhabitable shadow
triggers her fear-plundered heart.

Oyster Master Class

Laura Gamache

Our shells clacked on the plates
my tongue was a filling estuary.
—Seamus Heaney

Ostrea or Crassostrea, they are
filter-feeders with small three-chambered hearts.

Hama Hama, Little Skookum, Totten,
Hammersley, Potlatch and Belfair State Park—

Kumomoto and Pacific thrive, our
Olympias nearly harvested out.

Follow Linger Longer Road to Quilcene,
or drive to Lilliwaup, gather your own.

Push wedge-bladed knife into hinge where shell
halves touch, patience releases the oyster.

Be careful your blade doesn't buck. Your blood
and this bivalve taste equally of sea.

A Ballad for the Unclaimed Ones

Angel Gardner

I'll sing a ballad this once
for the unclaimed ones
because they said
the pastel-painted girls
with the holes in their lips
were without homes,
but beautifully wasted.

Fishnets ripped to stylish perfection,
cigarettes clamped between rainbow
bruised lips.

I'll sing a ballad this once
for the unclaimed ones
boys with patches on jean vests
and pulsing with nomadic urges.

Talent hidden beneath discrimination
with hearts in back pockets.
Called tough for actually feeling.

those boys,
were without homes

but
had I found my own
I never would have known it.

Driving Home from Spokane

Carolyn Gilman

The Inland Empire.
I don't really know it,
But I know the drive home.
A countdown of exits,
Two-seventy-six to one,
Prairie to timberland.

From the Palouse Highway
To I-90—from Cheney
Through Ritzville, then Moses Lake.
Each a pillar on the plains.
Tumbleweeds to the wide, flat
Columbia. Roll on!

A glimpse of iron horses.
We coast across the gorge.
Vantage. Ellensburg.
Let's play Name That Crop.
Two choices to tune in:
Country or mariachi.

Cle Elum—almost there
Passing in a moment
To trees, tall and blurry.
Green as high as you can see.
Water trickling from rocks,
Winding us home to the west.

Cold Nights

Sierra Golden

Fire unlit, I slide small blades through fresh
herring, thin ribs just a prickle as they crack,
flesh peeling into strips no longer or thicker
than my palm. Breath shivering out, shadows
scooping into a small circle of light, I layer
mason jars with onions, lemons, fragile white
fillets, and the bitter embrace of pickle juice
cooled in the dark. Peppercorns drift
as planets. Cloves comets. These cold nights,
the jar is the universe and I find its light.

Because It Is Waiilatpu,

Lenora Rain-Lee Good

After Tony Hoagland

the winds come through the valley
carry the death songs of those who lost

their blood upon the ground. You must be still
to hear their songs, and even then the words
are in a language only the dead can understand.

Because it is Waiilatpu, little
Alice Clarissa runs and tumbles, laughs

with the exuberance of a two-year-old toddler,
through the purple rye, to play with the other ghosts

not understanding their weeping, not understanding their death.

Because it is Waiilatpu,
covered in emerald grass, turtles nest by the mill pond
deer wander through the replaced orchard

winds carry the dust and grit of plowed fields
the perfumes of sage and wheat, grape and rye.

The ghosts use the winds and the grit to polish the marble slab
to high sheen, knowing when their names are obliterated
they will at last be free.

Because *this* is Waiilatpu.

Boy on the Beach

Joseph Green

He is playing by himself in the sand.
He wears glasses. He's maybe eight years old.
He makes tractor noises with his mouth
as he pushes the sand into place.
He uses a piece of driftwood to push it.
When a line of pelicans flies over him
he imitates the squawking of a seagull.
When he catches me watching him, he leans
in more closely to inspect what he is building.
He stops making the tractor noises.
He stops making the seagull noises.
He concentrates on shaping the sand.
But the tide has changed and soon the waves
are going to rearrange his excavation.
If I were to speak to him now I would say
Welcome, welcome to the life of the mind.

Shank

Sally Green

For Cora

Though she lives in a world of Velcro, snaps
and zippers, I'm showing my granddaughter how
to sew on a button. She's nine, same age I was
watching my mother pick my favorite one, shaped
like a flower a child might draw, color of sunshine.
Her homemaker hands held everything together,
needle and red thread lickety-splitting up, over,
down, up again attaching the blossom to grass-
green cloth: *Colors no bee could pass by.* Now, before
the last tug of thread through the button
my granddaughter brought me, I point out the pinch
of space—width of a scissor-blade—between it
and the fabric, a shaft of stitches with a half-dozen
twists of thread around it before tying off. *Shank,*
I tell her, same as Mother named it. It strengthens
the bond between button and garment, less
friction than ready-mades, fasteners that loosen
too soon. *Like love,* my mother said. *Close, but not too
close.* A snip of thread and my granddaughter's ready
to go, fluorescent-pink button back on the nose
of her dog-faced school bag, the shank fixing us
together in this world my mother could trust
only so long as everything was done right, only
when she didn't forget to check I was *buttoned up
proper,* buttoned up tight.

Belle de Boskoop

Samuel Green

For Chris Stern, 1950-2006

We were back a day from saying good-bye
to an old friend. I stepped outside
to fetch wood for the fire & heard
what sounded like shots or the angry door
of a truck being slammed over & over—
tree branches snapping under eight to ten
inches of the weightiest snow
we'd seen in our lives, thousands breaking
across the island. We lost limbs
from every tree in the orchard: plums,
apples, fig, cherry. The peach tree bent
in a long arch to the grass. Only the Boskoop
couldn't carry the load & split
at its crotch, the trunk a white wound
clean to the frozen ground.

Named for some Dutch village
beauty two centuries gone, we bought it
for how soon it came on, not so red
as William's Pride, not so good
in the cellar as Jonagold,
but sweetening with time.

While it snowed, our dear friend died.

When it thawed we used wood clamps
to force the trunk together, took an old tube
from a bicycle tire & stretched it 'round the bark
from grass to crotch, cut cedar braces to help bear
the load & called it good. Next summer we thinned
the fruit to lighten the weight. Clamps & tubing
came off in the fall. The scar was a jagged ridge
of bark, imperfect as our own healing
though we bore no outward mark.

Stares Like Pins

Jasleena Grewal

I passed a man wearing a weasel with
its face still on,
not from here or maybe
from Bellevue.

I wished him luck,
there were picketers down the street
waiting.

I gazed at my shoes, Converse still
new, and trampled them in the mud

sparing myself
from the glares, at least.

The Gates family
never wear snakeskins or
ferrets. Their estate
private, like the wealth
we accrue.

Cocooned in counterculture
lined by a silver dollar;

"Joan did five
mission trips, while
Jack did only one,"
we say.

In the speakeasy gastropub,
perched on artisanal toadstools

the weasel man walks by and we snigger.

Eagle

Mark Halperin

You look, and as if it had turned up out of the blue
and started eating just moments before,
it's there in the snowy field, not much more
than dark body and bobbing head, huge too,

and you think of the wild turkeys you've seen along
the road recently, flocks of them spreading out
into the countryside, and you're about
to turn away, when, with a few strong

beats, it rises on wings so long and broad
there can be no doubt it's an eagle, though which kind,
a golden, or a bald—still immature—

you can't decide, and while you're gawking, awed
by its size, its strength, the power of its climb,
it's higher and gone, obscure as pure azure.

Postcard, January 1922

Robert Hasselblad

Once we surrendered the homestead,
farther west seemed better.
No threading our way back
through the loss. We must
cede those dim years,
no need to varnish it. Just
own the failure, turn a page.

Winter's milder on this side
of the mountains.
Rain-sodden mornings
when he hunts work in town
and the girl's at school,
I relearn glory. Fill the stomach
of our shack with Bach.

Via Negativa

Irene Hayes

A spiritual path, one part of which is the discipline
of saying "no" to anything that is not yet clear
enough to warrant a whole-hearted "yes."

Building the bomb
was never a clear *yes*.
Not fear, but fascination
drove them—and desire for control.
They distracted and separated elemental particles,
sharpened precision triggers to strike just so.
A mind's playground where
those who laced our armistice with warfare
were used to making decisions
murky with maybe.

Testing the bomb
was never a clear *yes*.
Ordinary people
stood open to the elements
in southwest U.S. neighborhoods
or distant Marshall Islands.
Dazzled and blurred blind
with no apparent burn,
children, in waves of dust glitter,
swayed, coughed.

Dropping the bomb
was never a clear *yes*.
Thousands of heartbeats silenced
in a chasm of charred remains,
an irrevocable act—not inevitable.
Sheer wanton power out-blazed
our best intent,
that latent peaceful bent, once holy,
abandoned
for want of a whole-hearted *Yes*.

Building and dropping the bomb during WWII
were such a strong part of Richland culture that the
mascot of Richland High School was the bomber.

On Inviting Wendell Berry to Orting

Merna Ann Hecht

*In tribute to the farmers, gardeners, food bank workers and
volunteers of the Pierce County Emergency Food Network & FISH
Foodbanks of Pierce County*

Assure him it's Washington State,
not the other Washington,
Wendell has no use for beltways or outlaws,
tell him Orting is an ample place
plump with orchards and flourishing fields.

You will bring him to the Mother Earth
Farm, where his elderberry eyes
will grow wide as the orbs
of black-eyed Susans,
when he learns of this garden's good use.

Remember, he's already told us that
*to cherish what remains of the Earth
and to foster its renewal
is our only legitimate hope of survival,*
his kind ears are all ready
to receive a good story,
so tell him this:

> how the Mother Earth farmers grew
> tomatoes the color of midnight
> because women transplanted
> from Ukraine and Russia longed for them,
> how the immigrant women broke into song,
> when they tasted the dark
> honey of home.

And tell him this:

> that other women arrive here
> from a prison called Purdy,
> to plant and till,

until something shakes free,
takes root in the slow way
of the earth he knows best.
Do not look away
from his tenderness when he learns
of children brought to the farm
to stand with their mothers,
easy, without foreboding
glass to separate them.

Then lean in close
as he whispers softly,
advocates for kinder ways
are mostly unheard,
but hear him.

Next, is a side trip
to Tacoma, quick drive up Hwy 162
through Puyallup,
saving his crinkled Kentucky eyes
from the ruined speed of I-5,
head north so Wendell can take the hand
of a man with a Rip Van Winkle beard,
and a story as long as the semi-truck
he drives, huge and painted blue,
turned into a grocery store on wheels,
arriving at the same place
and the same time, like faith,
like prayer, like a rolling church pantry,
the offertory plate already filled
without obligation, and no worries
about how much is enough.

Sounding

Christine Hemp

Last fall the Silvers ran so thick, we cast
about for what was truly ours—what might last.
When the world tumbled from the sky, you landed
plenty of fish. I had one on, but lost it. Granted,
all this losing goes far. But absence
spawns another shape in its space. It moves
below the tide. I feel the depth charge. I'm getting up
my nerve to dive, even though I always have to shut
my eyes below the surface. I'm learning to trust
your fins and wings which offer more than a glut
of salmon or the splash and glittery commotion
I'm often lured to. I'm coming to a chosen
place where heat and coolness meet. Repose.
Two seals sunning like commas on the ice.

Pioneer Square Pile Driver

Rebecca Hoogs

For months, the pile driver drove.
It was a metronome
that passed the time by pounding it,
hammering home

each second like a nail.
For months, it beat its hard
heartbeat halfway to China.
It got inside my head.

It got my goat. The dust it made,
it got inside my bread.
Once I went outside to see
it wind and then drop dead.

The sound was followed by a ghost,
a little puff of dirt,
the pestle making
the mortar hurt.

A So-Called Respite

Christopher Howell

I.

The Portuguese taxi driver said, "Sailor,
Paolo knows just
what you want: a woman
who will screw your nuts off
for just fifty escudos."
I said it sounded painful, and he said
that all the great pleasures
were painful, that life itself would be nothing
if not for its beautiful pain.
I said, "Yes, I think that's so.
But I'd just as soon keep my nuts."

II.

It was Lisbon, 1969, and considering
what was going on in Asia, it was great
to have a northern European cruise
just at that time. But, in some ways,
it might as well have been Rome
in the time of the Republic
when the legionnaires were granted extended leave
after years and years of service on the ramparts
in Gaul. It being supposed
that a certain amount of wild carousing
would keep the troops in fighting trim,
all indiscretions short of murder
were ignored.

III.

The driver let me out at a place called
the Texas Bar in the alley next to which
a sailor was beating a marine over the head
with a wicker-bound wine bottle.
Inside, a wincingly ridiculous three-piece combo,
featuring an accordion, a tuba, and a flute,
entertained the drunken minions of the NATO fleet
with "Hey Jude." A naked woman danced
like a zombie on the bar.

IV.

Buffeted in the crush of reveling men
and incredibly friendly women, I spilled my beer
on a boatswain and he jumped up,
marched me outside
and pasted me a good one.
I slugged him back and we both stood there
bleeding. I thought about the Mekong and the armies
making the same history we were making
right there. I thought about pain,
and the boatswain bought me another beer.

V.

Somewhere around 1200 B.C., Priam
looking out over the plains of Troy
saw that true sorrow is the end of worlds,
that pain is how you know the end
has not found you, that something remains
and you are its soldier.

Women Glean Apples in Wapato

Penny K. Johnson

Your grandson   you say   a final chance
June he could graduate   only he isn't
all his past   Is it me you ask   am I
doing-it-all-wrong   What about

> *(2 green feed sacks: Sonya apples, the result of controlled
> breeding between Red Delicious and Gala apples are
> now grown in our volcanic soil of Washington State)*

my father   left my mother
seven children   North Dakota   to be
a monk   but then the priest kicked him out
Me the disaster when my first husband   stumbled
on a lucrative prostitute   All his problems about to be

> *(2 cardboard boxes of Golden Delicious: hybrid
> of Grimes and Golden Reinette, original tree grew
> Mullins' family farm Clay County, West Virginia)*

You would have thought I'd taken a crap
on the kitchen table   This family rips apart
like grackles   Picks skin to shreds   isn't there
just one   single drop of allowance   Only thing

> *(2 wild birdseed bags Pink Ladies: Cripps Pink
> Cultivar of Golden Delicious and Lady Williams
> a crossed blush of the sweetest graft)*

then you and I spawn the spawns   Entire
genealogy blissful as tadpoles   and   we
can't   finish it   I yell   use a chisel
razor to the granite   We can only
jam a stick in the spokes   This rear view

(3 boxes Granny Smiths: propagated from a chance
seedling, a hybrid of European Wild Apple with
domestic M. domestica as the pollenser)

right-this-second begins now for this grandson
Watch as he sets sail on   this-is-my-own-course
full sail ahead   he shouts   It-never-will-be-will-be
a write-in-ballot for a new direction   clear-the-way.

Our Glass Can

Isamu Jordan

Shake out the shine behind the gold pan
on a porch with an old man
My toes jam to a Sony Walkman
and a mix tape made in Japan
I keep my eyes closed wide
Swayin' to the beat like the tide
I hide in my head and confide in the dead and the wise
they said, never let 'em see you surprised up in the web
"Have another peace of cornbread, it's soul food
that when you digest and don't chew. Pay attention
when there's older people talkin' listen," he said, "Look
I done seen more than you...can read in a book
I spent life as a petty crook, straight crooked
And what I didn't give away, age took it."

And More Vivalding

Richard Kenney

1. Symphonic

March upcrumples expostulate sky
like a mongoose on a doily,
welcoming sun as thumb to eye,
while treating robins roily.

Green ferns bend a breeze
under summer's awning;
windows wide in libraries
and books and hammocks yawning.

Autumn whooms in fire first,
sumac, oak, and maple:
napalm bloom soon doused in mist,
and rain straight as cable.

Solstice doldrum, wool-chill,
the world in cold pajamas,
her icicles all prism-still
as air is, after hammers.

2. Redirect

What's the point of penning verse
like this? Why not erasures?
Something edgy, fresh, fierce,
on sex, or shame, or glaciers?

If we'll just slice the spinal nerve
the sun'll settle still.
It won't bank and swoop and swerve.
We'll study it at will.

That's good advice. Cerebral. Apt.
All rhyme I'll soon rescind–O…
I'd do it now, except I keep
glancing out the window.

The Bee Dancer

Larry Kerschner

The roofline is set
the new bee hut is square and level
open-faced to the southeast
when the bees arrive
in a few weeks
I shall dance a bee dance
of welcome
by April my bare feet
may be able to raise some dust
where now there is mud
intoning a poem about bees
my fat belly jiggling
over skinny legs
I will attempt to waggle appropriately
to show them the way

At the Ballard Locks Fish Ladder

Rachel Kessler

Do you think the giant squid
ever touches itself,
wandering a tentacle
in a documentary voice?
And it attacks one limb with another?

Not the best table topic for a couple
stepping into a mortgage.

Under the locks
the sea shifts a shoulder.
If only belief were truth!

A sardine is anything you get out of a can.

A couple walks into a house.
The spire stabs the heart
of the sun's deviled egg.
Be careful.
The algae is never gone,
the damp gropes under the house's blouse.

Is this the worst mistake you ever made?

Those that make it arrive in ragged condition, spawn
and die. It is hard not to be sad around salmon.
Fungus grows from their wounds.
If only the poem could turn here!

Fish are finding their way home with special nostrils,
U-turns of scent, back to the river of their birth.

Watch them leap, watch them batter themselves
against the rocks, watch them thrash through the air,
leaping arguments against compromise.

Olympic Harvest

A Haiku Sequence

Jason Kirk

daylight saving time
at ferry dock, daydreams rhyme,
take wing, fairly flock

polyglot folly:
hear not the melancholy
bebop of leaf rot

unlock words of rocks
and birds, non-stop jocular
interlocutors

in audible thrall
to the marbled call garbled
by all waterfalls

talented talons
of bald eagles maul even
the smartest varmints

claw marks in the bark,
warm cougar scat: cat's warning
maneuvers—true that

haggard dragonfly,
like a laggard dagger, poised
there in the moist air

three or four hours
of powerful peace beneath
meteor shower

under different
stars, dissident bard wanders
with cricket at large

Psalms from the Palouse

Shelley Kirk-Rudeen

Wind rustles knee-high winter wheat, still green.
Moves without a sound through shorter sprouts of grain
sown just this spring. Cloud shadows spill across the endless hills,
past solitary farmsteads, lines of trees for windbreak.
Barns and sheds. Trucks and combines. Plows and disks and rakes.

Sun shines on a mare's flank, the long legs of her foal.
Glints on three silos standing in a row and on the steel rails
for the train that will take the wheat away.
I imagine fields turning yellow in summer's coming heat,
workers bent to harvest, the dust and sweat.

Let this be remembrance each time I taste bread:
how fields rise to meet an empty sky arced high and wide.
The way coyote races wind-whipped grass.
Seed-heads swelling as they slowly turn to grain.
The lonesome farmhouse where sheets billow on the line.

Maple Grove

Laurie Klein

Manito Park, Spokane, WA

Hustle of edges—hear them?—
one leaf moving against another,
tissues juiced and swollen
with light, all the dappled coming
of hues barely withheld, quiescent
as scarves up a sleeve,
while into the trembling
canopy, clouds decant
champagne, and we kiss, blinded
to swarm: Ten-thousand mites
feast on these trees, secretly,
slowly, enfolded in growths of each canny
maple's making, grotesque little galls
weirdly bird-proof, immune
to swoop and peck, the smallest
talons on this most drinkable day
still goosing our throats, because
appetite begs accommodation,
you, me, all these peelerstar
trees and their bugs
moving deep within bark
primed for sugaring.

Slough Music

J.I. Kleinberg

After the painting "Salish Atlas #104" by Tyree Callahan

I am the slough, sluggish stream, earthmuck shore,
my shoulders a fresco webbed by mergansers,

my channel, poignant groove, carved trace of earth's
lust for water, my turnings and returns a kind of breath.

I am the clay, gray-silt slurry, mollusk-drilled, beak-scooped,
thickening the brackish soup of mountain's mineral memory,

slick-slipped alluvium, drenched sluice to scoured throat,
sun-sintered, to craze, crack, melt in the strata of seasons.

I am the sedge, ankled in glacier-fed cold, socked in algal green,
tickled by minnowy fry, by tadpoles browsing a splay of heron feet,

the dragonfly, delirious jewel,
darning shadows in emerald dashes.

I am light—moist, estuarine, riparian—feasting on riffled amber,
on tufted hummocks tinted gold, my hunger for the horizon prolonged, urgent,

raptor-shade a sumi swash on mudflat and marsh,
darkening comb through whiskered cattails.

I am reflection, color's sly glance upward into the maelstrom
of cloud, headlands, islands—my mirage pressed against the flesh of water,

armored scales bronze and brass, hue of sunlight fawn and flax
on sprawling pelt of animal earth, night in slow tarnish, umber and soot.

I am the bird. These are my fine bones, my feathers, my flight.
I am the chorus. These are my voices, the verses of my song.

These are my rhythms: chum, chinook, coho.
I am all of it. There is no I.

Tank

Sarah Koenig

I am a view into another place
and for that I must be cleaned
three times a day

the octopus shrinks into my corners
though there's really nowhere to hide

I don't think the jellyfish even notice—
embryonic, cerebral

who's feeding the fish anyway?
pellets fall to sand
as if they were falling asleep

the kelp thinks no one notices
its hula dancing
its delicate hips

I leave the top open to the light

in this way I leave things open
to interpretation

it is the sky you know
and it is not the same sky

Elders Rage at the Water Spirits After a Shootout

Robert Lashley

Reflection, on the lake
is a ripple that eats
then spits out an outline of the woods.
The women in black dip their old tambourines
then blur away from it.
The old men tie their suits into knots
then blur away from it.
The people join and move their hands
to deny his name in the cold.
    "The water spirit brought us."
    "The water spirit will not bring us home."
They wash the memory of blood in ice
and cry power in the darkness.
    "The water spirit will not bring us home."
Hums turn to shouts and chants rewoven
and moans play in scale with the squirrel bounce.
    "The water spirit will not bring us home."
Frogs jump a beat back from their hand claps.
Night bugs swarm but cannot trace steps
in an array of burying grounds
of shadows and spirits in the water.
The juba clap is the overriding veil
of sirens and funeral pyres.
The gun shot at night is the eleventh plague
so they part this iteration of the sea.
    "The water spirit brought us."
    "The water spirit will not bring us home."

Landscape with No Net Loss

Jenifer Browne Lawrence

This is the river's fingertip, pink bulb-end of a wild onion.
The sun leaps from the water and drops into the forest.
Bits of blown deer lichen float off without license.
I have changed a fuse in the dark. Have shoveled
trenches for cable, pulled the sway-end of a survey chain
until my palms blistered. I flirt with mosquitos in gray light,
wish I still smoked, stub my boot-toes at the marsh edge.
From the estuary, up comes the mist in faltering heat.
Longfin smelt change direction midair, belly-slap
to avoid the chinook or shake loose eggs
or just for the hell of it, who knows, we are all
bouncing off one body and into another.
On the map, or from the treetops, the river mouth
is a hand spread wide to catch everything.

Too Late

Jenny Liou

It was hot and he was old so I stopped. Half his teeth were
perfect, the others missing. Two of his fingers were
blown off at the knuckles—he had been a miner. He had
been in fights and quoted Robert Service who said
each fresh move is only a fresh mistake.
Had I been young when he was young I would have found him
handsome, which was an unfair thought—he was telling me about
cancer. He described ranches we would pass
in canyons receding from the road—
fragrant grasses, soils washed down from streams…
The Blue Mountains cast shadows in foothills
laced with trails ascending past them.
Those trails all led to houses, and he wished one were his,
wished he had spent his life so as to allow it.

Walla Walla Sweets

Eric Lochridge

Grandpa once chomped into the white layers
of an onion as if it were an apple.

Got a whole crate you could eat like fruit
they're so mild, he said, chewing a smile

then trotted back down to the dock
to prep another boat to sail.

We scattered his ashes there today, simply—
no funeral, no casket, no last hug or kiss,

no chance to lean into
the faint scent still wafting off his lips,

to breathe and carry year upon year
the essence of a life so sweetly lived.

Nisqually Delta

Priscilla Long

For Susanne

The wind is up, the sky cold blue
over the Nisqually mudflats.
Small trees poke through wave-
white froth, the flooding high tide.
Great blue herons stand motionless
as icons. Gulls sail blue air. Ducks
duck their heads into white water.
I would show this delta to you
who are dead by your own hand
30 years, but you cannot see
the wild sea nor hear croaks
of ducks nor your other sister
clumping joyfully along the long
boardwalk to McAllister Creek.
She marvels at dunlins flashing white.
Your toddler niece, now 33, points
to a bald eagle high on a branch—
a spirit messenger—so they say.

From GHOST TOWN, USA
Mill Plain Blvd. & Andresen Rd.
2/28/09

Christopher Luna

Upper-middle-class women and their mothers
     take Hummers to Safeway
to pick up poinsettias and birthday cakes:
you never know when you might encounter
     an Iraqi insurgent hiding in the dairy aisle
     or a tweaker with a Rocket-Propelled Grenade Launcher

Mt. Rainier

Vikram Madan

Mt. Rainier, Mt. Rainier, oh mountain of joy
The sight of you makes our heart skip
Your snow-capped visage looming weighty and coy
Keeps Puget Sound thralled in its grip

The reason you pep up our greying morale
Is one that can rarely be topped
Your sentinel stance, viewed across this locale,
Implies that the rain must have stopped.

Dungeness Valley

Ruth Marcus

1

Undisturbed morning view
landscape of granite gray
Olympic jagged peaks
meet lavender blue fields,
shoes wet from morning dew.

2

Barn owl poses in wooded scene
thick feathered coat
head bobs, turns on alert—
we stare, eyes in trance
morning wisdom in the air.

3

Ice-age memories tumble
in the swift water rapids
rocks bank the smooth journey
of Dungeness waters wedded
to the sand of Chetzemoka Beach.

4

Trio of crows soar and dive
over Railroad Bridge trestle
morning chill blushes our cheeks,
we listen as bald eagles
scold the trio

In Every Ripe, Ready Thing

Terry Martin

When I arrived, pumpkins dotted the fields.
Poems, too, were scattered about. I wanted
to gather them, and myself. Inside that cottage,
brimming days spilled over. I connected
with the window seat. My fingertips traced
lines in the table's grain. Hours and days
spiraled inward and inward and inward,
nested like Russian dolls. The wood stove
meant something to me. Stars pulsed
in the black sky, elemental and calm
and good. Vivid dreams spit me back to shore.
Each thing led me to another. Silver leaves
shimmered clarity. Chattering starlings
lifted into sky, wheeling south. Trumpet
vines climbed the trellis, striving from seed.
Bees buzzed hives, making wild honey.
In its own unruly handwriting, the wind
scribbled its message. I was a magpie,
collecting every scrap of color. I left,
having found what I'd been looking for.
Believe me when I say it was enough.

The Mountain

Georgia S. McDade

Mt. Olympus
Mt. Fuji
Kilimanjaro
Diamond Head
The Rockies
Everest even
the Cascades
all beautiful in their own way
I've seen them for myself.
But Rainier, "The Mountain," is my mountain.
I love that mountain.
The whitest of whites sometimes
a light brownish, golden tinge on occasion
a pinkish, strawberry tinge on other occasions
an ice cream cone where the ice cream is not too hard and not too soft but just right
freshly snow-covered, snow-covered, partially snow-covered—all different
always a pleasant and welcome sight and site
sometimes higher, sometimes lower depending on my location
(though I know folks who swear Rainier moves!)
seeing Rainier from commercial airplanes
flying around Rainier from a private plane
traveling there at least annually, taking anyone who'll accompany me
being not the least bit flustered if I have no company
traveling south on Rainier Avenue—despite another route being faster
thinking if I just drive straight I would drive to "The Mountain"
I never miss the chance to see the The Mountain.
Knowing The Mountain is out ALWAYS lifts my spirit.
When Mt. St. Helens exploded, I prayed Rainier never does the same.
I worried about volcano Rainier for a long time; occasionally I still worry.
This is my personal natural site.
While out of the country for six months, I often missed The Mountain.
(Some folks never crossed my mind.)
When I returned home in December, I had an eleven-day wait to see The Mountain.
And oh how glorious!
Mount Rainier, The Mountain I love.

52-Blue

Heather McHugh

And if I conjure up his image now, it is because
he calls like crazy to my heart, so long

deep-sixed. (He cannot get
his kind to understand

his wavelengths: They are deaf to him,
as he is deaf to me.) Their medium's a mixed

and hectic place: it thrums with human
commerces (subsonic, ultrasonic, supersensible)—

that's how we worry them, in peace or war.
It's all these gonged communities can do

to keep in touch with one another, without
listening for him, the hapless 52.

    *

Without companions at his side
to twine his tones in touch, can he

feel safe, or known, or loved?
Must he go on forever to explore

the corridors and the cathedrals of the sea,
past kelps and corals, shimmering and gloom,

feel forests with his tail, touch tunnels
with his tip, in hopes of finding, anywhere,

another like himself? Or only rarely,
as if in a dream, arrange to catch

that odd unfathomable glance—
a drift of silver, gist of blue—

a ghost, or god—whose partiality to him
now flashes from a mirrored room

inside a sunken ship.

Where the Sun Goes Once It Sets

Ross McMeekin

To Larsen's Bakery
in Ballard
for a slice of red velvet cake
and a Coke with bourbon,
maybe two,

and home to his wife
to make her giggle
until she joins him
in the bathtub
for a romp,

then to the couch
to smoke a bowl
and fall asleep
naked, with a bag
of Cool Ranch Doritos
on his chest.

He's going to do
precisely
whatever the hell he wants,
because goddamn,
he's been burning all day.

Starting Late in the Afternoon

Maureen McQuerry

You ask if there is time,
the sun already rides the horizon's shoulder,
these ridges we hike softened to flesh pink,
curvaceous as a sleeping animal.

I don't want to be the one to say
we must turn back, the shadows
are stretching and time dives
like the peregrine in a stoop,

to whisper no good can come of it.

Instead I say, watch the falcon
each muscle wages one intent:
to snatch a starling mid-flight. Maybe this
is what it takes, a sharp plummet
in the early dusk, all or nothing.

If we had anticipated the view from here,
we would have started years ago. Epochs
before us this sand was sculpted to stone,
cinder cones spit lava, and creosote bush
burrowed through scars. Our time

weighs less than the falcon's feather
and yet, what is time or age or coming dark
against night's first and burning star?

Ozette Beach

Catherine Alice Michaelis

I came for the whales: blue, humpback,
killer—I wasn't particular on this.

I came for myself, to cast adrift
fickled fortune and drop anchor

in mahonia, mugwort, salmonberry,
sea stacks nested with deer.

I came for the bleeding sun cut on the horizon's blue blade,
the bark of seals urgent in the dark.

Ozette, oh love, oh destiny,
oh ravens' *caw* against my sleep.

I knelt by the cedar longhouse,
shushed by waves that kissed the lip of my prayers.

Seven bald eagles climbed ladders of warm air,
oh Artemis, oh Pleiades, my cartwheeling heart.

About George

Kevin Miller

Your note ends with a question
and the photo of George, his eyes
follow something off camera.
Unfair advantage knowing G dies
wearing excuses like armor fashioned
from foil. I wonder if he believed
the money he owed would keep him alive
like overdue library books or the half
tank of gas he kept in the Plymouth.
Once he showed me his favorite picture—
the Saggy Baggy Elephant's belly
rising above the surface of the pond.
He kept his Golden Book buddhas
for safety if the voices refused to stop.
When I tuned his radio to a station,
he laughed, when I left, he found
the white noise I never understood.
Some days I miss his silly fears,
the manhole covers, the crows.
Their clicking call kept him wearing
the black hat indoors, his trick
to fool them through the window.
And the hat, we dropped it
from the bridge at Van Zandt,
proper topping for his ashes drifting
the Nooksack to Bellingham Bay.

Haplotype

Maria Rosa Mills

From an evolutionary perspective, it is bad business to breed dogs with wolves. Wolves are not incipient dogs, as we now know. The skulls of truly incipient dogs have been found in caves across Eurasia, mostly fractured; the whole ones fragile enough that transport back to the lab can be harrowing. These skulls belonged to what we term "wolf-dogs," though they are neither wolf nor dogs. Science has only a handful of these skulls. Perhaps the wolf-dog line split just before a glacial maximum, meaning many speciation details may still be buried in ice. Remember the winter we spent in Spokane? The gray wolf leaping lean through frozen pines? Its fur was like a sleepwalker in a white river. Statistically, memory means little to a wolf, and littler still to the modern dog, but the first true wolf-dogs made much of it. They began to come when called by name.

Spokane

Karen Mobley

Do not eat more than two fish a week from the river of murk. Bill the Fauceteer, master of old plumbing parts crowns with copper pipe. Tormino's Glass man makes seductive proposals while windows are measured. White's Boots steel the boots' toes. Miller's is unsurpassed in hardware. Someone here knows how to sing "The Battle Hymn of the Republic." Our state is named for George Washington, President of the United States. I don't know if his teeth were really made of wood. May Hutton was a suffragette. Mrs. Browne started theatre and all that shameful dancing. Lewis and Clark came by. Thompson explored. Cowley started the first church. In 1893, there was a wheat panic. The Great Spokane Fire burned the town. Mr. Duncan brought lilacs. In Manito Park there used to be a lion in a cage. At Drumheller Springs, Spokane Garry taught. There is a meteor hole filled with trash, and norovirus at the homeless shelter. A man digs up ant hills looking for gold. In Washington, the loss of grasping is worth more than in Oklahoma. $118,266. It says so on this chart. The French horn player says naked ladies are okay. Someone remembers what it means to be a tree. There are more than a few dogs named Jake. There is a place called Z Nation near here. The Monroe and Washington street bridges fell into the river. The governor was mauled by a bear. There are soldiers buried west of town near a place for those who wander downhill. Water is held in the cleft of the rock. In the old days, things were thrown into the river to wash downstream—sawdust, garbage, chamber pots, and offal. The Japanese Garden was built in 1961. Our children ride around town on metal goats and carousel horses going round. If you dig down, you might find the bones of salmon or Chinese in opium dens. If you turn carefully, you see the cursed ghost of Jimmy Marks or the naked ass of Willie Willey. Drink in the meth and the bootlegged whiskey. No, not all Indians make totem poles. Heron stands still through it all. Amen.

A Ghost Minority

Daniel Edward Moore

Some people come to this B-movie town
for how intense simplicity feels, for what it's like
to be extras in a world, drunk on beauty,
and sad they can't be more. Down on Front Street,
restaurants and stores border the Penn Cove shore,
where not long ago baby whales screamed
as their mothers were dragged away onto boats
to live behind glass until death. But they died then,
unknown to the world, in front of a camera's glass eye.
Oh, Coupeville, I'm only one percent
of eighteen-hundred minds, a ghost minority
telling the world what the majority won't.
Like why Pratt's feet in his grave point north,
to throw off the angels on judgment day
when they come for the Saints of Sunnyside.
And why he built a cabin for his boy to live in,
shielding his ears from the flesh he loved
through twenty-five feet of silence. Other unmarked
historical scars are not important now, not as important
as the words in my mind diving at me from a raptor's height,
like Alastair Reid's, "Islands seem to take revenge
on those who regard them as personal Edens."
I do not staff the Welcome Center to a world made famous
by mussels and clams, where anyone's likely to open and close
and find something missing inside, something smaller than a whale.

(Untitled)

Elizabeth Myhr

when we first met
you opened me like a letter

who can speak of what the peony gives out
when it's bowed down to the ground with rain

Dear Mr. Cooke

Arlene Naganawa

When we waited on you at IHOP
sunny side up, toast, black coffee
we knew you liked all of us, Jody
with her bleached blonde braid,
Luli and Janie's air guitars.
When we visited your apartment,
I envied the fireplace and leaded glass.
No photos, just a Chesterfield, chairs
and British knickknacks—porcelain
roses and turned candlesticks.
Mr. Cooke, I should have guessed
you set your clock on the bedside stand
in the dark, that you waited until seven
to take your usual table. I should
have thought about my father, working
graveyard shifts to pay for books
and my tuition, packing his sandwiches
in wax paper, drinking from a midnight
Thermos of hot tea. I used to like a cigarette,
standing in the propped back door
with the busboy who became the one
I broke my father's heart for, hitchhiking
to Nevada. Mr. Cooke, I'm sorry I didn't
admire your books in their leather covers
or take you to fireworks at Green Lake.
In the papery aftermath of family picnics
we could have watched from a blanket
cascading waterfalls and peonies,
silent last chrysanthemums.

How to Run Above the Cliffs

Shankar Narayan

Allow honesty
enough. Of Olympics, of sea. The same run
always different. Blood on a difficult hill
when she is old. Straw-shorn fields dark
matter. From the persistent
third world with her mongrel
and '57 Ford. Approaching upright
stained red with infinite goblets. Find love
for a land never yours
entirely. Compassion your heart
exploding. Into the ventricles
and auricles and other
empty spaces. Who runs the places
you once did. Of temple bells half a world
away. Of your upturned blue-veined
love. Aspire to pace
your billion cells all your truths

persisting. Cup the one
you pass. In shore-surf
rings at the perigee
of your approach fragments
of lives all around. Kindness
and strangers that burn and burn.
Of wine. For something for no one
taking air from your endlessly cycling
footfalls. Mountain and sea
and distant sails. Eyes of salt lagoon—
ears of donkey-Buddha.
In your ear Nusrat
exalting. What breaks and breaks
and regenerates when you no longer can
run. Her kohl-eyes
the hill. Rip your chest
like typhoons through empty.
Running

you miss her. The strangeness of kinds
these greening yards
those loving palms. Of beast. Your eye
the corner of an unfamiliar field. Virtues
of silence and wandering. Who desires to reside
in hollows of your left lung. Sense the deer
sensing you. Let you nearer and nearer then
lightning bolt—to river running
to ocean running always away
from you. Hills burning
into ragged lungs—who
sings the torn note
you once embodied. That smile.
Find someone's second sight—see
deer mountain sea sun
gleaming—a tooth a fang
something animal something
of your heart
these lavender views

97. Clues from Hell

Paul Nelson

Smoke rises to heaven when it ought to descend to hell.
–Ramón Gomez de la Serna

& a heaven's of yr making a home be it the Rock or Careladen, Woodtown or the Lake, Ka'gean or Cloud Nine, Slaughter or a little corner of Hillman City survivable by p-patch. Make it w/ enough care to notice from the lichen to the day moon. From the library to the Japanese maple. From the giant sunflowers to the three-steepled cedar points to better weather.

In it & in the chaos of the marked-up books, the three-toed vase, the empty Otokoyama bottles in the recycle bin, clues. To sift through the wreckage one day they'll want clues. Clues to how you ended up next to a fire (well-tended) & clues to the spiritual chase. Clues to the record & direction (for future seekers) & clues to where you hid the Humboldt Fog. Clues cd hide right in front of you as does the sponge plant by the duckweed drift which smears the morning Lake. Clues of cigarette butts & grief.

> Old growth redwood
> 800 years old
> 300 feet tall
> heard its share
> of prayers.

They were always there we'll say, prominent as miniature islands w/ salal, blue huckleberry & dwarfed spruce. Calm as the Lake ripples made by a coot flock landing. Subtle as the woodsmoke rejecting hell in the making of its new home as it courts the morning Cascadia fog. Sincere as autumn bouquets (sweet little nosegay-like) for every dead stranger in the cemetery made w/ the spirit of great cobwebs of geese in the sky & mild-mannered hallucinations of reverse snow in September Olympic fireweed or the hush of dropping fir needles w/ each new exhale from Blue Glacier.

So stock up on cake mix & tequila, butter & turkey bacon. Mangoes y pan de banana. Have handy jasmine rice & altar candles, fresh garlic & olive oil. Cashew bits & blush wine. Wool socks & binoculars. Photos of the loved ones & always the clue-enabling ancestors.

Decoding the sea
& the heavens
ain't for sissies.
Lend a hand
or stand back.

4:08 p.m.—N.8.13
The Lake
Loleta, CA

All quotes from Morris Graves

Influence

Sierra Nelson

At the bottom of Lake Washington there is a train
sunk with the barge that carried it, train cars still filled with coal.

Seven airplanes, including a four-propeller World War II bomber,
bomb-bay doors open, .50-caliber machine guns inside.

About 400 boats, including ferries, barges, three Navy minesweepers.
Some sank in fires. Some in storms. Some got so old the owners sank them.

Bags of garbage. A body of a dog tied to concrete.
A baby in a bag, research.

Two drowned forests. A village.
Our gifts were not a wooing.

Sleeping Woman

Duane Niatum

She was a woman who fished in dreams for herbs
and plants on the healing path.
The village children last saw her at the mouth
of the Dungeness River.
They were watching salmon return from the sea.
The elders said she was the salmon's guardian
and when she sang they would leap as if calling her name.
The children round-danced and stepped lighter than joy.
Sleeping Woman, whom they met on the river path,
promised before the next rising sun she would sing
to them of a forest flower that smelled
of mystery, family, and seasons, yet remained
a secret of earth and forest.
Her song flowed through the hollow of their bones.
The children felt larger than life and leaped
into the sky with moon moths.
Sleeping Woman, stepping softly beyond them,
veered in and out of light and dark and cedars,
disappearing in the rolling-back wave of the moon,
a deep swirl of planet and star.

Searching for the True Name of the Douglas Fir

Sheila Nickerson

These are the trees we take
for pianos and violins,
the ones we sometimes steal for guitars.
We know their music but not their name.
Certainly it cannot be "Douglas fir"
(no fir). Nor can it be "Douglas,"
no matter how brave the young traveler
was who sailed here to claim their seeds
and take them back to Scotland.

The name must be magnificent:
wind in the tall masts, symphonies,
Steller's Jays haranguing in branches—
so magnificent it can't be said;
and that is why taxonomists have
struggled so and failed.

If only we would drop our needle
words and let the trees enfold us,
we could know what trees know:
that bark and skin are one
and language, tangled as a forest,
cannot always lead us home.

Run Out of Stock

Courtney Oldwyn

We bought three burlap sacks of horse feed,
sent them to Standing Rock in the back of an island farmer's rusted blue pickup.
Comanche Nation, Northern Cheyenne, Choctaw, Puyallup, the Yavapai-Apache
entrenched under a North Dakota winter sky, two hundred years into the same fight.
She didn't want their ponies to get hungry.
So Natives were on her mind when
during November's Applesauce Feast
(organic Waldron Island Honeycrisps from a classmate's orchard)
she asked me if Old Grandma Penny was really an Indian.
Half-Cherokee, I explain,
though she envisions only
pilgrims, wigwams, and painted horses.
Seven years old, blue-eyed, skin golden as a hayfield in August,
she knows nothing of trails of tears,
Wounded Knee, the Little Big Horn,
Chief Joseph's last stand, the lost language of the Lakota-Sioux.
Yet she rides—
my wild-haired daughter, face up toward the Great Blue,
thick-thighed like her daddy,
barefoot on a blonde pony.

Another Angle

Kristen Orlando

In the river that flows through the river
is the pink-scaled shimmer of salmon—
mothers on suicide missions,
frantic with full bellies,
looking for deliverance,
drowned out by the hum of flies
whose sonic reverberations
rustle the cat's tails of October—
there where there is still enough sun to angle,
enough light to cast,
you spot shadows in the water.

You remember what he told you when you were young
and more interested in rolling on the thick grass carpeting the banks
than walking into slippery rocks.
He said, river shadows keep certain things in the dark.

Underneath the rush you know there are stones that have worn the water
for as long as the water has worn them.
Round as bellies themselves, they are waiting for you.
This is where you stop and reach deep.
You have held this stone before.

Cold from the river, water running from your elbow,
you bring it to your mouth.
It is always the same river. It is always the same stone.

You put the stone in your mouth and wait for what the water will deliver.

Boom

Nancy Pagh

Along cliff edges we walked, above beaches tossed with yellow cedar
broken free from booms. Driven ashore by storms, tugged and nudged
by tides into monkey paws of the high-water line, they silvered. "Dig in
your toes," Dad said. Single file. Hold hands.

grain of sawdust
grain of sand
time drifts
time lands

White-frosted cupcakes, a flask of milk, waxed-paper cups, pulp napkins.
The remote picnic table was split gray wood, patina'd. If you paid attention,
you noticed an old chain attached it in place.

strong links
home
fitted words
poem

Marine Science Center, Port Townsend

Shin Yu Pai

after an hour of exploring
indoor touch tanks with our son,

my husband signals he's ready
to move on, though our two-year-old

lingers unready to plunge
a hand into cold pools or to go

home, he'd held back Kort's hand
from touching the spiked orange

sea cucumber, buried his face
in our arms when a crab sidestepped

nearer, but regarded the colorful feather
duster worms with a closer curiosity,

that made me question the urge
to survive, instincts that no longer

serve a purpose yet keep us
from pushing out beyond the comfort

of the cocoon, hands clasped
together, I watched my partner

ease our child's palm into sea
water to come into contact with

the purple tentacled tube worms
fan-shaped appendages pulled

back in a flash, fear transforms
into surprise, delight repeating

itself again and again, as our son
grows bolder with each reach

May 18th, 1980

Carl Palmer

near to a year remains in my tour before the date to rotate back to the
states my family with me serving the U.S. Army stationed in Hessen West
Germany before the fall of the Berlin Wall witness white ash fallen on our
blue BMW blown across the Atlantic Ocean from Mt. St. Helens blowing
her top in western Washington USA over 8000 km away where we have
orders for Fort Lewis Washington wondering how far this military base
is from the base of that erupting volcano covering stubborn Harry Tru-
man of Spirit Lake Lodge like Pompeii from Mount Vesuvius along with
other hazards we heard had occurred in this earth quake shifting-plate
region of the upper San Andreas Fault where yet another stubborn
soul Tubby the three-pawed dog biting rather than abiding his would
be rescuer from atop Galloping Gertie Bridge caught by a west coast
hurricane-force wind sent tumbling down into Puget Sound's year-round
40- degree waters where the world's largest giant Pacific octopi reside not
more folklore like the famous humanoid bipedal Big Foot a.k.a. Sasquatch
roaming the Washington rainforest with wild herds of two-legged Rainier beer deer or legends of Tacoma's secret unfound underground tunnels burrowed beneath skid-row streets for waylaying drunks from seedy
seafront taverns to sober up as shanghaied sailors aboard merchant trade
ships anchored offshore in Commencement Bay in 1885 or those Point
Defiance secret caves hiding ousted Chinese during the Tacoma Riot that
same year not at all unlike the Japanese internment of 1942 to concen-
tration camps outside this grit city calling itself T town, city of destiny
32 miles south and always in the shadow of Seattle home of the 1979
NBA Championship Supersonics and the Seahawks squad with gridiron
matchups played in the SoDo cement Kingdome loudest stadium in the
NFL sharing Seattle Mariners home games whose class A farm club the
Bellingham Baby M's became the Tacoma Tigers renamed the Rainiers
of Tacoma's Cheney Stadium in 1995 that same year as the Toyota Tacoma pickup truck was put on the market and debut date of the downtown
district makeover making blue-collar Tacoma an urban cultural experi-
ence with a free passenger trolley connecting points of interest along
Pacific Avenue to and in between the renovated Theater District neighborhood and Freight House Square around the corner down from the
Tacoma Dome built with 1.6 million board feet of Douglas fir harvested
from the Mount St. Helens eruption on May 18th 1980 near to a year
before the Army moved us here where we make our home in Tacoma.

On the Chehalis River

Lucia Perillo

All day long the sun is busy, going up and going down,
and the moon is busy, swinging the lasso of its gravity.
And the clouds are busy, metamorphing as they skid—
the vultures are busy, circling in their kettle.

And the river is busy filling up my britches
as I sit meditating in the shallows until my legs go numb.
Upstream I saw salmon arching half into the air:
glossy slabs of muscle I first thought were seals.

They roiled in a deeper pocket of the river,
snagged in a drift net on Indian land.
Trying to leap free before relenting to the net
with a whack of final protest from the battered tail.

They'll be clubbed, I know, when the net's hauled up
but if there were no net they'd die anyway when they breed.
You wonder how it *feels* to them: their ardent drive upstream.
What message is delivered when the eggs release.

A heron sums a theory with one crude croak; the swallows
write page after page of cursive in the air. My own offering
is woozy because when their bodies breached the surface
the sun lit them with a flash that left me blind.

For Li Po

Paul Piper

My words have fallen into the moon
which has fallen into the water.

Should I rescue them?
I think not.

We are all allowed one phone call.
I chose you.

You are what the moon sees
when it looks up.

Communion

Anna Quinn

There are days when the only antidote
to the crazy is a walk to the fish market
the one in the commercial boatyard
because you need the clamor and pound
of things built, things painted and fixed

your mouth asking for a pound of halibut
the fish guy in the black hoodie and red apron
lifting the entire fish from the ice
placing it on the scarred butcher block
hacks off a good-size chunk
the heft of that cleaver!
sets the fish silver side down on the scale
Asks: Fifteen ounces okay?
Yes, you say.

He wraps it like a sacred thing in white paper
you count out two fives and three ones
and carry the white package
to your little tug and climb inside
fry it in butter, two garlic cloves, a bit of dill
pour yourself a mug of wine
and when you lift the first flaky white
to your lips, you close your eyes
stick out your tongue, and
say, amen oh my god amen

Coroner's Report

Ben Read

In 2009, a dead man sued Toyota
because he said the acceleration was stuck

and he fell into a ravine. Coroner's report:
he never pressed the brake.

In a field near Cheney, the wheat dissolves
into locusts. Nowadays boys kill themselves

with bridges and guns and cars, synonyms
for men. And aren't bodies automobiles, taken

over by roots? Heart as rusted engine, I ran
towards the moon, alabaster sliver, a grin

of teeth. Sky in gradients of turquoise.
It takes ten years after going blind

for the body to stop dreaming of sight.
The moon waxes in hope, wanes

with desperation. I can see him,
foot on the gas, white smile,

falling like the rock I threw, that landed
short of the river. Accelerate.

I count graves like miles. Out here,
the night air is warm and the stars are more

than dreams. The locusts rise
to eat them whole.

Colonel George Wright Shot 800 Horses Here

Laura Read

After the painting "The Indian Wars" by Kay O'Rourke

I am a fish and a girl and a ghost, hanging
in the sky. Without my clothes,
you can see my bones picked clean.
Beneath me a brown horse buckles
under a brown man. Beneath me blood.
I used to believe the dead were just gone,
but I am not the only skull in this sky.
Remember how you and Annie played
with her plastic horses on her living-room
floor and they turned the rug into a field
they ran across, their hard manes flowing?
Annie's house was always dark and her parents
filled it with silence. Annie came over
every morning to walk with me to school
or swim team, and sometimes my mom
stepped out of the bathroom and there was
Annie in her thick glasses and chlorinated hair.
In 1858, Colonel George Wright shot
800 horses at Hangman Creek, not far
from here. Every day I drive to work
down Fort George Wright Drive.
Sometimes history is as close as my hair
blowing in my eyes. A horse's muscles
shift under his skin like a kind of light.
Like the way Annie could swim,
lap after lap ahead of me, her body rolling
so perfectly when she did the butterfly
that everyone stopped to watch,
and when she got out, our coach
wrapped her gently in her towel.

The Things We Carry Now

Philip H. Red Eagle

For Tim O'Brien

It has been 25 to 30 years, or so
      since we neatly folded up those
      greens and blues.
Put away web belts, brass buckles
      and medals of many colors.
Nothing really.
Memories locked tight
      and safe.

Yet there are these things we carry with us;
      To help us through hard times.
      Treasures of sorts.
Useful things that serve a purpose,
      like before.

There's this little two-inch lock-back.
      Pretty little thing.
Good for slicing divits
      and cleaning under the nails.
Not a Buck,
      or a K-Bar, but useful still the same.

Here's a mini-Maglite, double, or triple-A.
Mini-foldup scissors,
      band-aids for some cuts.
A little silver matchbox
      and a compass,
      just in case.
A coffee cup of stainless steel
      It won't break, or rust.
Shoes that will take me anywhere.
      The soles were made to grip.

These aren't exactly issue,
        but they do me just the same.
They're right here when I need them,
        and they keep me through the day.

Out front I wear these shades,
        So no one can look in
        and see the man
        born of loss and pain.

Inside I wear a little darkness
        the color of that wall
        Blackness like a mirror
        and full of the names of friends
        and relatives

My life is made of little things,
        borrowed from a life ago
        when things were tough and gritty
        and I was young.

This Is Why the Relationship Might Work

Susan Rich

Because the call of shorebirds wakes me
and this morning I watched a seagull

sunbathe on a wine-colored Camaro.

Because the air offers up notes of saltwater
and scrub rose whenever I walk out the door

even if I'm on the way to the grocery store.

Because the wine, because Walla Walla—
and Hendrix. Because we travel

by ferry and the world's longest floating bridge.

Because flocks of joggers along Alki Beach
nod a quick hello like gold finches

keeping apace to the beat of black wings.

Because tumbleweed and tulip—
fish ladder and the Looff Carousel—

because we have declared an official oyster.

Because hemlock, because humans who plant
sungold tomatoes and build boats from cedar and oak.

Because I picked you from all 50 states

to be my valentine of sweet
onions and jazz apples. Because the rain.

Because someone chose a piece of petrified wood

for the state gem—and because without
the journey out West, we would never have met.

Heidi

LeAnne Ries

You drive us out to the L.T. Murray, to your inheritance: a string of radiators and rusting pickups, shotguns behind their seats. You say that's your favorite part, finding them there, still loaded just like in 1984 when John used to head out to buy a load of tires or make a loan. We go down the line, pushing the seats forward.

Go back forty years to 1974. You and I bring a brown paper bag from B. Dalton's into your room, hide the *Happy Hooker* under your bed. When it's really late and your parents have gone to sleep, I will read the dangerous words. You will hold the flashlight. After you nod, I will turn the page. I read faster than you do.

Today, I tell you to keep the bailing wire to make a sculpture for your mom's garden: a few plants just outside the door and some bulbs by the clothesline. One kitchen chair. We cross the road to find wild acres of dead junk, cars planted in the soil. Detroit fenders settle in for the long haul; my hands will go before they do, thin skinned, bones already showing.

Palouse Falls

Katrina Roberts

I saw once the shoulder of a man long petrified, bone
to basalt, saw where he'd reclined alone against sky to become
an undulant line called horizon, inscribing within a word a world.
I saw through glass what must have been his strapping thighs-
become-tablelands long after the repast, littered with a random barn,
a silo or truck, a combine abandoned, and I thought them nothing
but a shaker for salt, a pitcher a giant striding through could lift
to pour out. Our pretty doll-sized fences were ribbons, mere
gestures, to pin brief and often petty stories to a corn-hued shawl
draping the shorn earth's enduring bones. Dusty red, a Martian-
scape channeled by dripping fingers of some Pleistocene god. Did
he spin first with compass-arms outspread to encircle this plateau,
as a brindled hound, echo-wheeling to find somatic bliss turns, rapt
before finally sinking down into his own weathered skin? The scab-
lands go on for hours. So many scars. Legend says four brothers
chased Big Beaver, aimed keen spears at the creature (damned and
damming) four times, each thrust gouging to wound as they
wound in thundering pursuit past a scraped-knuckle butte, past
a tufted expanse of bunch-grass licking the hilly expanse north
of the Snake, each needling a tattoo on canyon walls; Appaloosa
manes streamed a wake of black staves the notes of a keening song
could barely hang on to as they rode, until a fifth blow tore a jagged
rift in the fabric trail they galloped, let loose the river, and sent it
tumbling over. *Aput, Aput,* falling water, falling still. My white
Ford a transient iceberg drifting, drifting nearer. I might drive high
plains all morning, lulled and unsure what will rise past a bend, then
see a hundred acres more or less the same. A crow flying would
have been there already. Silence. Dry, snaking road. Then, a mirage?
No, a promise. The sign! An empty lot, my door swung open, still
nothing. Then, traipsing twenty steps to the trailhead, I see: this gut-
dropping chasm (nearly 200 feet), no guardrail at all, to the coulee
floor where a bright vein throbs, gleaming to fill the sweltering
cavern of August. What keeps me from stepping off? The heart-
stopping cool of a glacial torrent, where craggy switchbacks end,
calls, despite loose, precarious rocks. I could sit in the deepest place,

strip my binding socks. How often it's like that, right?—so little
warning with the cataclysmic. What seems a wide horizon as far
as eyes can see, what seems inevitable—the pieced quilt of an heir-
loomed life, the managed trajectory of health, a marriage, however
shiny or filled with daily drudgery or grief it might be, suddenly giving
way, the bottom simply falling out. That summer day, before turning
to drive back home alone, I tipped my face to listen to unlikely tongues
of pure water breaking themselves to pieces without emotion, without
joy, nor fear, nor lament, without grudge nor knowledge there'd be
any confluence downstream, traveling surely who knows how far nor
fed by which distant springs, only rushing to plummet so easily over
the staggering torn lip of land, over and over again, simply giving in
to delicious gravity, to make for me the most delicate lace veil.

Stick Indians

Tom Robbins

You'll never really see them
and there's nothing left behind
to identify them in the labs
    of DNA.
And that footprint beneath your window
where in the night you saw a shadow
of a shadow of a shadow on the pane?
Just a heron with a gimpy leg
or some scarecrow run away
    to search for love.

When the owl suddenly freezes
on its perch atop the fir,
little ears cocked like nacho chips
    waiting for the cheese,
you yourself will listen hard
but only hear a scratching,
a clawing and a rasping
of the wind that wants to jimmy
    your locked door.

It's said they're a tribe of hermits
(whoever heard of such a thing?),
professors from the university
    of mud.
On paths of old mischief
they steal down from the hills,
bird nests for moccasins,
broken twigs like scratchy vowels
    spelling out their names.

While anthropology prays for day
to break and bring an end to nights
    it can't explain,
you have to ask, "Where are they
then, and are they any different
    from the rain?"

Well, they seem to have an interest
in all the things you do
when you suspect no one
        is around.

And somehow you know they're out there
beyond the porch light's reach,
in the brambles,
in the hedge,
out behind the woodpile
where they certainly appear
        to feel at home.

You imagine them raw and willowy,
you picture them splintered and dry,
you imagine them witch brooms
        come to life.
But no matter how you picture them
or joke that they're your friends,
you can't begin to grasp the shtik
        of stick.

The Stick Indian casino
is in your skull
—and you've already lost.

Attenuation

Janette Lyn Rosebrook

The Hanjin Geneva is paralyzed in the Pacific.
Come home.
The whales can't eat the goods in your belly.

Come home, Rebecca Moss,
the sea is not your residency.
Even the squid knows how to escape
the comedic situations created when mechanical systems
and nature collide.

Even the old salt knows,
as he tramps along the seawall,
his stilted words
a Morse code,
his arms—
waving maritime flags
in the morning wind.

Lucid Ruse

Rob Schlegel

On the train, I whisper-recite Spicer: This ocean, humiliating in its disguises / Tougher than anything. / No one listens to poetry. The ocean / Does not mean to be listened to. Toxic fog enhances the scene for Big Ricky filming crows eating coyote beside tracks near White Plains. According to the stranger behind me this is where Nico drove his Monte Carlo into Jealous Kelly. Big Ricky pulls his shirt over his face. Wipes the sweat away. Not enough deodorant is what his eyes seem to say. Now he's watching *Star Wars*. The voice promising, "Together we can rule the galaxy as father and son," also promises, "People will come. People will most definitely come"; Terrance Mann's baritone like butter over milk toast dipped in dreamy fields of Iowa corn syrup against the Lord Vader raising his hand one or two seconds after his verbal command. Impossible to sync Jones' voice with the body of an actor grasping for authority from behind a black mask, hilarious in his disguise. You can almost see his pedigree. Someone's ringtone's robotic voice announces *That idiot is trying to reach you on your cell phone device.* Everyone struggles to stay relevant. In 1878, Thomas Edison proposed to equip the Statue of Liberty with a disembodied voice that could be heard from midtown where twenty vendors is ten too many for Met Security, rich and lasting fact of shaking hands sanitized compulsively. In the museum's labyrinthine bowels, dead elevator shafts contain pools filled with koi. Though it's no one's official job, they're fed bagels from 9th Avenue where police dismantle toasted Everythings. In his apartment, nearby, Jeff conceptualizes a microphone system by means of which, one's voice emanates from a point slightly above, or to the left, or right of one's mouth via speaker indistinguishable from a large mole or beauty mark. Genre's dissolve is describing the rest of the day. The sound as such that evening is not mine. Boiling water for tea I smell Aldehyde. Google says leave. We evacuate. Kisha calls me crazy. At least no one is hospitalized is me rationalizing the irrational gorged sick on my overactive imagination because writing poems is the kind of crazy that could find me some future Thursday: Cosmic Night at UBowl, pins aglow in black lights dilating my sacral dimples nearby boys turn to see. Insert fingers here, I'll say, and ruin me down this lane. Not because I suspect the world is ending, but because the fulfillment of this prophecy is only a poem away.

Solstice Song, Stevens County 2016

Lynn Rigney Schott

Unlike the way water
   walks on water
saving only itself
   the wind agitates for change
scatter-brained trees   leave
   on impossible missions

Mingo Mountain has been up
   all night listening to
the stuttering speech of the rain
   hold the truth too tight
it struggles to lie
   down in its nest of words again

The great flat foot of winter
   walks in the door
we must celebrate, sing something new
   beat out a difficult dance
like a heart in a wineskin
   you know   it's time to begin

A Catalogue of Things Given Up

Betty Scott

I love my children in cursive when they vow
they'll never switch and twitch with naked rage,
nor ever smoke, especially dope, nor climb out
windows inflamed by love to "ooh" and "ah"

at fireworks. I love my children in cursive, though
they say they'll never have kids, never donate
their laps to "Mommify more brats." No, they won't
read them books or answer to "What's dat?"!

When they text, grade schls teach typng
for the internet, not tracng curvs of letrs
2 stdy famly histry in dsty jurnal ntrys,
I go dizzy, unbox Grandma's nest of ledgers,
fall inside ancestral journals, and hug the embers
ashes sparking inside me, letter by slanted letter.

What We Hold On To

Heidi Seaborn

Dungeness Spit, Washington

The road gathers the fields, harvesting them with each turn.
A barn with silver silos crests the green horizon.
The houses, whose gardens snap sunflowers, rhubarb,
lettuce and stunted corn are the dream
we each harbor in the folded wing of our palm.

We stem from forest trail to the beach,
skid the sand between our toes,
feel the smooth circles of stone beneath our feet.
This spit is the crooked finger calling the ocean home,
the arm holding our family together.

We sleep on the driftwood,
eat cheese and sausage on Russian rye,
search for agates like four-leaf clovers.
The wind is not enough to unbalance the cranes from their post,
not enough to push us further down the spit to the lighthouse.

Blast and Surge

Derek Sheffield

After Robert Frost, at a gathering of scientists at Mount St. Helens

Some say blast
is what happened here.
Some say surge.
From what I've tasted
of dust-deviled ash,
I'm with those who favor blast.

But if it had to happen again
and again through the age
of the earth, I think I know
enough of heat
to say that for delete
surge is also
just a word.

What does it mean? asks one
as we stand upon a plain
of gray rock and look up
to a steaming crater.

Behind us shrubby trees
make patchy surges
of creeping return.
As they crisscross the air
around our knees, grasshoppers
click their yellow wings.

They mean to find each other
and breed in the heat
we mean to stop making.

At the Bybee Farms U-Pick, North Bend, Washington

Martha Silano

Where I plunked blueberries into a blue bucket,
leaned into the first bush on the path,
my daughter loping ahead, convinced
the best ones are further down, running
to show me five in her hand: See? What
did I tell you? But I couldn't stop picking
what was in front of me, though arguably
smaller, though barely able to discern
her red sweatshirt, her whole being enveloped
in green. Picked for an hour before fatigue
and boredom set in. Hot, hungry, starving,
dying of thirst: her litany of suffering.
We have to pick more, I said, though mostly
she cartwheeled, stood on her hands,
asked me to count, to watch, asked and asked
and asked. Half an hour more, I said,
then lugged our buckets to the stand.
13.68 pounds. Enough for a winter,
to fold into batter, fill a pie, though it was difficult
to imagine a day in December, reaching
into the freezer to taste July, white-crowned sparrows
pecking in the grass where I'd tried to convince her
the best fruit's where you're standing,
not at the end of the row.

Your Scars

Judith Skillman

You must wear them as if they were
fancier than imagination.

Think of silk organza pressed with design,
sewn together in rows of tight stitching.

You must allow them to malinger.
If you cut them off like the friend who told you not to call

they grow deeper and longer, tighter than a channel
carved from ice each spare summer.

That long-sought-after Northwest Passage
for lack of which a British captain's men
turned on one other, became cannibals.

Those men used what appeared to be weapons—
knives of bone, the peripheral flesh cut away
(fingers and toes)

to yield broad expanses of muscle-meat,
stretching out in every direction like Arctic snow.

Legends Say

Kathryn Smith

The maps furrow the palm. They vein a varicose thigh. If you'd been born here. If you'd been born. If your father worked graveyard and told your mother, just a few hours' sleep, and he dreamed the saw's whine while she breathed through each contraction. If the maps broke when they stripped her veins and the bleeding wouldn't quit. To squelch or stanch or stop a rock-bound river. To dam the blood and its antibodies, a river's platelets and plated fish. To unbox a collection of antique plates and find hidden there a photograph of your mother holding a child you've never seen, its fish-face gasping. If you'd been born as wood is split, the sawmill crying. If you'd stopped your ears and hadn't heard the foghorn, the ferry horn, the lady of the lake's tragic story. If you'd looked to your palm and chosen another path. If the trails were marked. If the sign read 1,000 miles to nowhere: Head due west.

What Remains

Ed Stover

The gathering shadows
of a warm summer evening—

the after-dinner dishes
washed and drying by the sink—

Mother, my sisters and I
pushing off for town in the old Chevy—

the roadway pale as bone in the moonlight—

the water tower at the milk plant
rising to the stars—

the air soft through the open car windows—

the smell of earth, hay and mint,
offal from the slaughterhouse—

the Star-Lite Drive-In,
figures moving on a big screen—

the dark line of the Rattlesnake Hills—

the glow of Mother's face,
her hands on the wheel as we turn into town—

the lights of the ice-cream shop,
sitting in the car licking cones—

finally, Mother's voice soft as evening—

Your father is gone;
he won't be coming back.

Legacy

George Thomas

Beneath my sons and me the ferry shudders in black water.
Seattle's hill of lights expands at our approach.
Two days back in a pass in the North Cascades,
We'd felt the wind, the peaks above the silence,
And winding up to meet us, the serpent road. Now
My youngest stands spread-legged at the iron bow rail,
The wind of passage sprays his hair and whips his jacket.
I know he thinks he is the captain of this ship.
Night bell of a buoy clangs in the dark around him,
His eyes stare into that hill of lights ahead,
His frame moves across that face of light, his frame
Which moves with the motion of this ship.

Drinking Beer at the Goldendale Demolition Derby

Joanna Thomas

Goldendale, WA
Monday, July 4, 2016

whop whop whop of
flapjack tires if you love it
lube it under the hood a
spark then smoke then oops
a flame full-blown phoenix
rising orange metal wings,
hot hot '86 pontiac firebird
get the hoses boys half-
naked chick yelling from the
bleachers her belly button
blue stars and stripes guy
neck red next to me his
tremendous belch rainier
erupting and everywhere is
dust

Point Hudson Light

Sallie Tierney

She sails stale bread off the dock,
watches it swell and sink
before the gulls can swoop
it up. Logs bump together like otters
as the tide turns, the surface
shifting from pink to gold
going black and still she stands,
stiff fingers grasping
an empty plastic sack,
her eyes following flight paths
of gulls outward bound
for Whidbey Island, her mind
following them past the nets
at the mouth of the bay,
out to the deep fissures
west of the cape—anywhere
but the single-wide mobile
where her man deals cards
to three strangers, deals
bad hands from the bottom,
throwing it away like fish guts
into a white wake, saving
only the anger for her
as darkness swallows her whole.

Bold

Anastacia-Renee Tolbert

she says the mouse is domesticated because it
comes out to eat when she is eating breakfast (sunny side up)

because it washes his hands & waits for her to say grace
because it walks around each trap & avoids eating pellets
because it knows when she is trying to kill (it)
because it won't just die already like everyone else
because it wants to live its life in her kitchen

like she's all bright yellow & sunshine

Smallpox First Came to the Pacific Northwest in 1770

John Whittier Treat

Written with Thom Gunn's poem, "To a Friend in Time of Trouble"

It finds it has lost itself upon
the smooth red body of a young madrone,
I built my home long ago among the Madrona trees
from which it turns toward the other varying shades
on the brown hillside where light grows and fades,
my home is on a brown hillside not everyone can climb
and feels the healing start, and still returns,
my window's view of Mount Rainier reminds me I came from elsewhere, whole
riding its own repose, and learns, and learns.
Your names, at first a few and then many, are lost to me in this home.

Memorial

Emily Van Kley

Planted after my grandparents'
war, the oaks
fend Legion Avenue,
seven decades undesecrated
by saw or pruning shear.
Trees don't mean
to mean anything, but death
demands a symbol, doesn't
it?—having no color
or outline of its own.
Root-heavy, they conform
to character, coerce sidewalks
to salute the sky.

       *

In high school, men
in butter-colored uniforms
summoned me from class.
Their dead were old, unlike
the dead of current wars.
I rode in their vans
to the cemetery,
unpacked my battered
coronet.
They presented
flags, their half-turns
precise, arthritic.
I was old enough to want
to sound mournful,
my aperture brittle
in fall winter spring cold.
There was one key to press,
one note to follow,
no one being called.

*

In winter the oaks make
a great show of sturdiness,
holding up armfuls of snow.
But this January the sky
flubs protocol, sends down
ice thick as ermine
to sheath and snap
branches at the crosshairs,
the road soon
such a giant's briar
it's a week before
the bus can pass.
Workers cinch
trunks with spraypaint.
Come spring
the city sends
climbers in matching
vests to stump
the trees, one by one,
crown to ground.

Ahem

Nance Van Winckel

: your throat-clearing tugs open
the bald barista's good eye
like the door to a tomb. Grande
Americano, how you'd long
been known, with a murky bill
unfolded from a crevice into which
this formerly mop-haired boy
once nodded gravely.

Precipitate

Connie Walle

Sasquatch lumbers across
the sky dark and menacing.
Squats low over the mountains
dumps snow and ice. Then
pisses on Highway 90, confusing
the drivers. We shake our fist
and shout it's fall you lummox.
It's golden-leafed picnics and
sunny-day football. He roars
with laughter, flashes a smile,
walks across Puget Sound
to Purdy and Allyn.

Rain into River

A rengay by Michael Dylan Welch and *Tanya McDonald*

dark clouds—
the ferry's wake
whitens the ocean

> *between bay and sky*
> *the gold of maple leaves*

pinking sunrise—
the jogger's altered path
by the overflowing lake

rain into river...
a flash of blue
as the ruddy duck dives

> the puddle muddled
> by red rubber boots

silvered with dew,
the spider web
on a sand pail

Masters of Condescension

Ellen Welcker

Masters of condescension—join me
for I'm about to monologue about MY TOWN:
a place I've lived for going on four years.
So expert am I at seeing the forest
for the trees, why, I unearth meaning
the way some people find geodes! My vision
so clear and all-encompassing as to be capable, nay
excoriatingly precise at summing up MY TOWN.
MY TOWN has grown men riding tiny bicycles.
MY TOWN has beautiful architecture. MY TOWN has real
live Indians, and a place called Hangman Creek.
MY TOWN has art people, runner people, subsistence
hunter people, Google people, meth people,
and ?? people. MY TOWN is near the white
supremacist town, but not too near it. MY TOWN
reminds me of the town I grew up in: the tall pines,
the raging fires. MY TOWN is better than that other
town I lived in, the one with the dead center
and the rattlesnake den, the chain-smokers
in the apartment below, and the heat shimmering
off the parking lot. I am not a lake person, but MY TOWN
has a shit ton of lakes nearby, so there's that. The lakes
are near or just past, some of them, the white
supremacist town, but MY TOWN's embrace of lakes is—
do you like rivers? MY TOWN has the most glorious
cold green river. On its banks there are "don't eat the fish"
signs in English, Russian, Salish, and Spanish.
I'm totally guessing on those languages. MY TOWN
has a little bit of a heavy metals problem. MY TOWN
had a fake black person, for real. She's gone now,
and I'm not totally clear on the reasoning
behind why MY TOWN is "a great place
to raise kids," nevertheless: affordable housing, moose
that sometimes saunter through the neighborhood,
a mural with both nudists and marmots on it,
and a couple of good, I mean really good breweries.

Naked People I Have Known #34

John Whalen

A nudist even in winter, Nelson is the kind
Of heirloom apple—Cox's Orange Pippin,
Bramley's Seed, Ashmead's Kernel—that warehouses well
Until it doesn't, and when the last box is shipped to Fargo,
I have to wait until fall for fresh apples.

That is, Nelson—sweet Nelson who says what I could
Never say—who is honest and naked and tan—appears
Everywhere until he doesn't. He's gone. And I begin
To understand his nakedness in relation to my own struggle
To speak in tongues.

I have a big problem saying no. A problem with anger
And envy and jealousy. Let me just say that
When Nelson is at the Shop at his corner table,
Perching on that chair with three legs, I can always
Point to him and say, I have clothes, don't I?

I am a man who owns clothes. Look at Nelson
With his bony, naked knees, and all that extra flesh.
Look at Nelson, his gray-haired testicles, so pathetic.
His stomach there for all to see. He never holds it in
Or feels shame. I am a man with a closet full of sweaters,

Though none fit. None are in a color I like. Forgive me,
I don't know what color that would be. Let's not forget
Nelson's bare behind. Who's going to sit in that chair
When Nelson gets up? Will someone come from behind
The counter to sanitize the ancient, varnished wood?

Oh, I am a man with a closet full of sweaters and mistakes,
Full of grievous sins and regrets, failures and defeats.
A man who has never seen in the mirror what is so simple
For everyone else to see. I have a little trick that helps
When things go dark. I place whatever it is that has stopped

Me with its barbed-wire hug—like I said, anger, jealousy—
Envy at another's success—debt—no success of my own
To block the razor wind—I set envy on an invisible platter
And lift it to the light, and I let go. I imagine the light burning,
Cleansing, envy to gratitude. Gratitude to peace.

Winter Saturday

Katharine Whitcomb

Last night I lay down
in front of the gas fireplace like an old dog
and fell asleep on the rug.

How long had it been,
what miles flown over full-speed, since sleep
seeped in, a warm fog.

The day for once bore
no schisms, no battering-rammed doors leaned
askew on their hooks.

A forest carries quiet
like cloth in its arms. When I was a girl I dreamed
this inside my books.

Great Uncle Erwin

Bill Yake

Ferry County, WA

Let cold leaves shuffle and fall.
September 1932 and a tree
kicked back on Erwin
who's extended his labor as investment,
favor, or repayment. Near Hoodoo Canyon
quick death smashed his skull. Expectations
that had named his mine Cuba,
a dream of galena,
extinguished—
"a perfect vein" the local news
had claimed, "of silver and lead…
a four-foot lead…that may widen
to eight…"

Oregon Mist

Judith Yarrow

"Oregon mist," my father said
of these gray mohair days.
"Missed Oregon, hit Washington."
And he'd laugh and feed another cow

while I fed horses
and thought to myself,
"How silly." But we both knew
the joke was worth a laugh.

The air, half water,
that we breathed, made us
as evergreen as boggy fields
and forest lots.

Sometimes he'd yodel
when the mood was on him,
though he said he hated farming
and would rather fish

than milk a cow,
or sow a field, or birth a calf.
They were fishermen,
his father's people.

It was in his blood.
And there he was wet-landed,
raising cows and kids
and dipping jokes out of the air.

(Untitled)

Maged Zaher

As you are sending gifts to nobody in particular, the small exaggerations you made all your life flicker and terrify you.

I was looking for a room without a world attached to it when you showed up.

Some devices need little electricity to bloom. Each day I justify my madness. I call it exhaustion. Now there are fewer things I can offer you.

The Doctor Asks Her to Describe It

Maya Jewell Zeller

Our hollowed brains
bump along these halls
like buoys, or like deer

    lain down by a tree
    when the day's last light
    folds to a crease.

        It's spring, so antlers
        are soft like velvet,
        easily broken like skin,

            easily sanctioned by men
            who need healing, whose
            bodies want to be held

                by other bodies. I've
                read what can be done
                with their head-bones:

a whole village healed
and more babies.
I am only part monster.

    Part of me is a woman,
    a home for your disease
    or what you imagine

        disease to be, a window
        you fear too much to pull
        open. I have grown

            to fear the glass, too,
            and what lies beyond,
            even the dark forest,

where before this,
trees seemed kelp-like
in the breeze. It wasn't

so different: a leaf
riding wind currents,
taking its time, insects

or lichen, moss or its
tiny spores that resembled
plankton or a human

reproductive organ.
Look, by now I've learned
how I sound. It's like

your boat crashed
on this island, I'm the only
option to keep you

from floating away alone.

Acknowledgements

Irene Hayes's "*Via Negativa*" is printed with permission of the author. Special thanks to Martha Swedlund for assisting with the text.

Isamu Jordan's "Our Glass Can" is printed with permission of the author's family. Special thanks to Jess Walter for providing the text.

Lucia Perillo's poem "On the Chehalis River" is presented with permission. It originally appeared in *The Bellingham Review*, then in Perillo's book, *Inseminating the Elephant* (Copper Canyon, 2009), and again in *Time Will Clean the Carcass Bones: Selected and New Poems* (Copper Canyon, 2016).

The editor would like to thank Humanities Washington and Arts Washington for their support—especially staff members Julie, David, Eric, Ellen, Glenda, Lisa, and Karen: you guys are like family. A big thank you to Sam, Kathleen, and Elizabeth. All three of you gave me great encouragement and advice; trust me when I say that your work is remembered fondly throughout our state: you helped people make songs.

A big thank you to my actual family on the West side of the Cascades for continually offering lodging and meals (and a never-ending supply of smiles from my nieces and nephew when they found out that their uncle Tod was staying over yet again). Am grateful to have old friends who encourage my literary endeavors—Nance, Rik, Ryan, John, Scott, Ann, Dan, Beth, John, Linda, Nicole, Jeff, Robbin, and so many others—as well as new friends throughout the state—Claudia, Amanda, Mark, Pat, Judy, Luther, Jane, Ed, Connie, Nancy, Elizabeth, Chris, Toni (to name only a few). Brian: I am glad to have such a good friend.

Lincoln, Laurel, and Zelda–!. Henry—thanks for being Henry; bonus perk of this gig was how often we'd hang out in Cap Hill. Teddy—I know you've missed me (but not half as much as I've missed you). And Amy—dearest Amy—no matter how long the road, all of my travels were okay because I knew you'd be there for me at the end of the journey. Love you lots.

Contributors

Sherman Alexie	Seattle
Luther Allen	Everson
Elizabeth Austen	West Seattle
Terry Bain	Spokane
Quenton Baker	Seattle
Julie Baldock	Enumclaw
Akesha Baron	Seattle
Dawn Pichón Barron	Olympia
James Bertolino	Bellingham
Linda Bierds	Bainbridge Island
Jennifer Boyden	Friday Harbor
Anita K. Boyle	Bellingham
Allen Braden	White Swan
E. Hank Buchmann	Ritzville
Catherine Bull	Seattle, Steilacoom
Jennifer Bullis	Bellingham
D.S. Butterworth	Spokane
Becky Carlson	Spokane
Bill Carty	Seattle
Claudia Castro Luna	Seattle
Joanne Clarkson	Olympia
Kevin Craft	Seattle
Mary Eliza Crane	Duvall
Michael Daley	Anacortes
LLyn De Danaan	Shelton
Alice Derry	Port Angeles
Pat Dixon	Olympia
Rachel Eggers	Seattle, Spokane
Lynne Ellis	Seattle
Susan J. Erickson	Bellingham
Laura Falsetti	DuPont
Leija Farr	Seattle
Kathleen Flenniken	Seattle
Mark J. Fuzie	Yakima
Cate Gable	Nahcotta
Tess Gallagher	Port Angeles
Laura Gamache	Seattle
Angel Gardner	Seattle
Carolyn Gilman	Olympia

Sierra Golden	Maple Falls, Seattle
Lenora Rain-Lee Good	Kennewick
Joseph Green	Longview
Sally Green	Waldron Island
Samuel Green	Waldron Island
Jasleena Grewal	Bellevue
Mark Halperin	Ellensburg
Robert Hasselblad	Tacoma
Irene Hayes	Richland
Merna Ann Hecht	Vashon Island
Christine Hemp	Port Townsend
Rebecca Hoogs	Seattle
Christopher Howell	Spokane, Vashon Island
Penny K. Johnson	Ellensburg
Isamu Jordan	Spokane
Richard Kenney	Port Townsend
Larry Kerschner	Centralia
Rachel Kessler	Seattle
Jason Kirk	Seattle
Shelley Kirk-Rudeen	Olympia, Spokane
Laurie Klein	Deer Park
J.I. Kleinberg	Bellingham
Sarah Koenig	Seattle
Robert Lashley	Bellingham
Jenifer Browne Lawrence	Poulsbo
Jenny Liou	Clarkston
Eric Lochridge	Bellingham
Priscilla Long	Seattle
Christopher Luna	Vancouver
Vikram Madan	Bellevue
Ruth Marcus	Sequim
Terry Martin	Yakima
Georgia S. McDade	Seattle
Tanya McDonald	Woodinville
Heather McHugh	Port Angeles
Ross McMeekin	Lake Forest Park
Maureen McQuerry	Richland
Catherine Alice Michaelis	Shelton
Kevin Miller	Tacoma
Maria Rosa Mills	Renton, Seattle
Karen Mobley	Spokane
Daniel Edward Moore	Oak Harbor

Elizabeth Myhr	Seattle
Arlene Naganawa	Seattle
Shankar Narayan	Seattle
Paul Nelson	Seattle
Sierra Nelson	Seattle
Duane Niatum	Seattle
Sheila Nickerson	Bellingham
Courtney Oldwyn	Friday Harbor
Kristen Orlando	Fircrest
Nancy Pagh	Anacortes, Bellingham
Shin Yu Pai	Seattle
Carl Palmer	University Place
Lucia Perillo	Olympia
Paul Piper	Bellingham
Anna Quinn	Port Townsend
Ben Read	Spokane
Laura Read	Spokane
Philip H. Red Eagle	Tacoma
Susan Rich	Seattle
LeAnne Ries	Yakima
Katrina Roberts	Walla Walla
Tom Robbins	La Conner
Janette Lyn Rosebrook	Bellingham
Rob Schlegel	Walla Walla
Lynn Rigney Schott	Kettle Falls
Betty Scott	Bellingham
Heidi Seaborn	West Seattle
Derek Sheffield	Leavenworth
Martha Silano	Seattle
Judith Skillman	Newcastle
Kathryn Smith	Spokane
Ed Stover	Yakima
George Thomas	Vancouver
Joanna Thomas	Ellensburg
Sallie Tierney	Burien
Anastacia-Renee Tolbert	Seattle
John Whittier Treat	Seattle
Emily Van Kley	Olympia
Nance Van Winckel	Spokane
Connie Walle	Tacoma
Michael Dylan Welch	Sammamish
Ellen Welcker	Spokane

John Whalen	Spokane
Katharine Whitcomb	Ellensburg
Bill Yake	Olympia
Judith Yarrow	Seattle, Tacoma
Maged Zaher	Seattle
Maya Jewell Zeller	Ellensburg, Spokane